Taiwan's Political Status: A Future as a Renegade Chinese Province or an Independent Country

Copyright Page

TITLE: Taiwan's Political Status: A Future as a Chinese Renegade Province or an Independent Country

1ST Edition

Copyright @ 2023

ISBN: 9798223146360

Taiwan's Political Status: A Future as a Renegade Chinese Province or an Independent Country?

By Roberto Miguel Rodriguez

The Future of Taiwan: The Renegade Chinese Province or an Independent Country

Political Status of Taiwan: Should it remain a renegade Chinese province or become an independent country?

The political status of Taiwan has been a contentious issue for decades, with differing opinions on whether it should remain a renegade Chinese province or become an independent country. This subchapter aims to explore the various perspectives surrounding this topic, taking into consideration the views of diplomats, economists, strategists, educators, historians, and the general public.

The debate over Taiwan's political status is not merely a matter of semantics, but a complex issue with wide-ranging implications. On one hand, those in favor of Taiwan remaining a renegade Chinese province argue that it ensures stability in the region and maintains the fragile balance of power with mainland China. They believe that reunification with China would bring economic benefits and access to a larger market, as well as greater diplomatic leverage on the international stage.

On the other hand, proponents of Taiwan's independence argue that it is a distinct entity with its own government, military, and constitution. They emphasize the importance of democratic values, human rights, and self-determination, asserting that Taiwan should be recognized as a fully sovereign nation. They argue that independence would allow Taiwan to maintain its unique cultural identity, pursue its own foreign policy, and forge alliances with other countries.

The economic future of Taiwan is a crucial factor in this debate. As a renegade Chinese province, Taiwan has benefited from its economic ties with China, which is its largest trading partner. However, the growing tensions between the two sides raise questions about the sustainability of this relationship. If Taiwan were to become an independent country, it would face challenges in terms of establishing new trade partnerships and maintaining economic stability. However, it would also have the opportunity to diversify its economy and pursue global trade agreements independently.

Furthermore, Taiwan's political status has a significant impact on its diplomatic relations with other countries. As a renegade Chinese province, Taiwan faces diplomatic isolation, with only a few countries recognizing it as a separate entity. However, if Taiwan were to become an independent country, it would have the potential to establish formal diplomatic relations with other nations, expanding its international presence and influence.

In terms of national security and defense strategies, Taiwan's political status is of utmost importance. As a renegade Chinese province, Taiwan relies on its own military capabilities and support from the United States to deter any potential aggression from mainland China. If Taiwan were to become an independent country, it would need to reassess its defense strategies and potentially seek alliances with other countries to ensure its security.

The issue of cultural identity also comes into play. As a renegade Chinese province, Taiwan faces challenges in preserving and promoting its unique Taiwanese culture in the face of Chinese influence. However, if Taiwan were to become an independent country, it would have the opportunity to assert its cultural identity on the international stage and safeguard its heritage.

In conclusion, the political status of Taiwan is a complex and multifaceted issue with far-reaching implications. It involves considerations of economic stability, diplomatic relations, national security, cultural identity, human rights, and democracy. The decision of whether Taiwan should remain a renegade Chinese province or become an independent country will have profound consequences for the future of the island and its relationship with the rest of the world.

Historical background of Taiwan's political status

Taiwan's political status has been a subject of contention and debate for many years. Understanding the historical background is crucial to comprehend the current situation and potential future scenarios.

The roots of Taiwan's political status can be traced back to the Chinese Civil War, which took place from 1945 to 1949. After the defeat of the Republic of China (ROC) led by the Kuomintang (KMT) in the war, the Communist Party of China (CPC) established the People's Republic of China (PRC) on the mainland. On the other hand, the ROC government retreated to Taiwan and continued to claim to be the legitimate government of all of China.

For decades, Taiwan, under the rule of the ROC, maintained a separate political system and governance from the PRC. It developed into a vibrant democracy, with its own constitution, government institutions, and military. However, internationally, there were varying degrees of recognition of Taiwan's political status.

Until 1971, the ROC represented China at the United Nations and held a seat on the Security Council. However, due to changing global politics and the rise of the PRC, the UN recognized the PRC as "the only legitimate representative of China" and expelled the ROC. Since then,

Taiwan's political status has been in a state of limbo, with most countries recognizing the PRC as the legitimate government of China and having limited official diplomatic relations with Taiwan.

The "One China" policy further complicated Taiwan's political status. This policy, adhered to by most countries, including the United States, recognizes the PRC as the sole representative of China and does not officially recognize Taiwan as a separate country. This has constrained Taiwan's ability to participate fully in international organizations and engage in diplomatic relations.

Despite these challenges, Taiwan has managed to thrive economically and become a global player in various industries. It has forged unofficial diplomatic ties with a few countries and built strong economic partnerships worldwide. Domestically, Taiwan has made significant strides in human rights, democracy, and cultural preservation, solidifying its unique identity.

The future of Taiwan's political status remains uncertain. While some advocate for Taiwan to remain a renegade Chinese province, others argue for its recognition as an independent country. The outcomes will have profound implications for Taiwan's economic future, international relations, security, cultural identity, human rights, social integration, economic cooperation, technological advancements, and environmental sustainability.

Understanding the historical background of Taiwan's political status is crucial for diplomats, economists, strategists, educators, historians, and the public to analyze and contribute to the ongoing discourse surrounding the future of Taiwan.

Current political dynamics and debates

The political dynamics in Taiwan today revolve around the ongoing debate regarding the island's political status. Should Taiwan remain a renegade Chinese province or become an independent country? This question has far-reaching implications for not only the people of Taiwan but also for the international community.

For diplomats, the future of Taiwan is a matter of great importance. They must navigate the complex web of international relations and understand how Taiwan's political status impacts its diplomatic relations with other countries. The question of whether Taiwan should be recognized as an independent country or a renegade Chinese province greatly influences its standing in the global arena.

Economists and strategists closely analyze the economic future of Taiwan in light of its political status. They weigh the opportunities and challenges facing Taiwan as a renegade Chinese province or an independent country. Economic cooperation and trade partnerships with other nations are vital considerations that shape Taiwan's economic prospects.

Educators and historians delve into the intricacies of Taiwanese culture and the preservation of its unique identity. They explore how Taiwan's cultural heritage can be promoted and sustained in the face of its renegade Chinese province status. The progress and challenges of human rights and democracy in Taiwan are also topics of great interest to this audience.

The integration of mainland Chinese and Taiwanese societies is another key area of discussion. In the event of Taiwan becoming an independent country, social integration becomes a critical consideration. How will these two societies come together, and what challenges will they face in the process?

Technological advancements play a crucial role in shaping the future of Taiwan, irrespective of its political status. The island's technological prowess has the potential to drive its development and enhance its global standing.

Environmental sustainability and conservation are pressing concerns for Taiwan. The impact of its political status on its efforts to promote these goals cannot be overlooked. How can Taiwan continue to prioritize environmental sustainability in the face of political uncertainty?

In conclusion, the current political dynamics and debates surrounding Taiwan's political status have far-reaching implications for diplomats, economists, strategists, educators, historians, and the general public. The future of Taiwan as a renegade Chinese province or an independent country has wide-ranging impacts on its diplomatic relations, economic prospects, cultural identity, human rights, social integration, technological advancements, and environmental sustainability. Understanding and addressing these dynamics and debates are crucial for charting the path forward for Taiwan.

Arguments for Taiwan as a renegade Chinese province

Introduction:

The status of Taiwan has long been a subject of debate and contention. This subchapter aims to explore the arguments for Taiwan as a renegade Chinese province, highlighting the various dimensions of its political status and the implications it has on different aspects of Taiwanese society.

Historical and Legal Basis:

One of the key arguments supporting Taiwan's classification as a renegade Chinese province lies in its historical and legal background. The Chinese Civil War resulted in the division of China into two separate entities, with the Communist Party establishing the People's Republic of China (PRC) on the mainland and the Kuomintang

(KMT) retreating to Taiwan. From a legal standpoint, the PRC claims sovereignty over Taiwan based on the idea of Chinese reunification.

Economic Opportunities:

Taiwan's status as a renegade Chinese province offers unique economic opportunities. Being closely connected to mainland China, Taiwan benefits from its proximity to one of the world's largest markets. This proximity allows for the establishment of trade partnerships and economic cooperation, which can result in significant economic growth and development for Taiwan.

Cultural Identity:

Despite its designation as a renegade Chinese province, Taiwan has developed a distinct cultural identity over the years. The preservation and promotion of Taiwanese culture in the face of its renegade status is an important aspect of Taiwan's identity. Embracing its unique cultural heritage allows Taiwan to strengthen its national identity and differentiate itself from mainland China.

Democracy and Human Rights:

Taiwan's political status as a renegade Chinese province has contributed to the progress and challenges of democracy and human rights. Unlike mainland China, Taiwan has embraced democratic principles and has made significant strides in protecting human rights. Maintaining its renegade status allows Taiwan to continue its path towards greater democratic governance and respect for human rights.

International Relations:

Taiwan's political status impacts its diplomatic relations with other countries. As a renegade Chinese province, Taiwan faces challenges in gaining formal recognition as an independent country. However, it has managed to establish informal relationships with many nations, and its participation in international organizations showcases its potential as a responsible global actor.

Conclusion:

The arguments presented highlight the complexities and implications of Taiwan's status as a renegade Chinese province. From economic opportunities to cultural identity, human rights, and international relations, each aspect has its own set of considerations. Understanding these arguments is crucial for policymakers, diplomats, economists, and others interested in the future of Taiwan. Only through a comprehensive analysis can a well-informed decision be made regarding Taiwan's political status and its place in the international community.

Arguments for Taiwan as an independent country

There are compelling arguments to consider Taiwan as an independent country rather than a renegade Chinese province. This subchapter explores the various factors that support Taiwan's pursuit of independence and the potential benefits it could bring to the country and the international community.

First and foremost, Taiwan has developed its own distinct political, economic, and social systems over the years. It has a vibrant democracy, with free and fair elections, a robust civil society, and a strong commitment to human rights. These foundations set Taiwan apart from mainland China and make it a natural candidate for statehood.

From an economic perspective, Taiwan has become a powerhouse in the global market. It is home to numerous high-tech industries, including semiconductor manufacturing, information technology, and biotechnology. As an independent country, Taiwan would have the ability to negotiate trade agreements and establish economic partnerships on its own terms, enhancing its economic potential and opening up new opportunities for growth.

Taiwan's political status also has significant implications for its international relations. Currently, only a handful of countries recognize Taiwan as a sovereign state, due to pressure from China. However, as an independent country, Taiwan would have the ability to engage more freely with the international community, forge diplomatic relationships, and participate in international organizations. This would not only benefit Taiwan but also contribute to regional stability and global cooperation.

Furthermore, Taiwan's pursuit of independence is closely tied to its cultural identity. Taiwanese people have their own unique language, customs, and traditions, which have been shaped by their history and interactions with various ethnic groups. As an independent country, Taiwan would have the opportunity to preserve and promote its cultural heritage, ensuring that it thrives and evolves in the face of its renegade Chinese province status.

Lastly, Taiwan's political status is closely linked to its national security and defense strategies. As a renegade Chinese province, Taiwan faces constant military threats from mainland China. However, as an independent country, Taiwan would have the ability to establish its own defense policies, strengthen its armed forces, and forge partnerships with like-minded countries to ensure its security and sovereignty.

In conclusion, the arguments for Taiwan as an independent country are multi-faceted and compelling. From political, economic, and cultural perspectives, Taiwan has the potential to thrive and contribute to the international community as a sovereign state. Recognizing Taiwan's independence would not only benefit Taiwan but also promote regional stability, economic cooperation, and the preservation of cultural diversity.

Implications and potential consequences of each scenario

As the debate over Taiwan's political status continues, it is essential to consider the implications and potential consequences of each scenario: whether Taiwan remains a renegade Chinese province or becomes an independent country. The outcome of this decision will have far-reaching effects on various aspects of Taiwanese society and its relations with the international community.

First and foremost, the future of Taiwan as a renegade Chinese province or an independent country will significantly impact its political status and diplomatic relations with other countries. As a renegade province, Taiwan's participation in international organizations and its ability to negotiate bilateral agreements may be limited. On the other hand, if Taiwan were to establish itself as an independent country, it would have the opportunity to forge its own diplomatic path and engage with the international community on its terms.

The economic future of Taiwan is also at stake. As a renegade Chinese province, Taiwan can benefit from its close economic ties with mainland China. However, it may also face challenges and restrictions imposed by Beijing. Conversely, as an independent country, Taiwan would have the freedom to pursue its economic interests and establish trade partnerships with a wider range of countries. However, it may also face economic isolation and potential trade disputes with China.

The impact of Taiwan's political status on its national security and defense strategies cannot be overlooked. As a renegade Chinese province, Taiwan may be vulnerable to increased military threats from mainland China. On the other hand, as an independent country, Taiwan would have the autonomy to strengthen its defense capabilities and forge alliances with other countries to ensure its security.

Cultural identity is another significant consideration. Taiwan's status as a renegade Chinese province poses challenges to the preservation and promotion of Taiwanese culture. However, as an independent country, Taiwan would have the opportunity to assert its unique cultural identity and protect its cultural heritage.

The progress and challenges of human rights and democracy in Taiwan are closely linked to its political status. As a renegade Chinese province, Taiwan may face limitations on its democratic institutions and human rights. However, as an independent country, Taiwan would have the freedom to further develop and protect human rights and democracy.

The integration of mainland Chinese and Taiwanese societies is a critical aspect to consider in the event of Taiwan becoming an independent country. The potential for social integration and harmony, or potential conflicts, will depend on the approach taken by both sides.

Lastly, Taiwan's political status will influence its efforts to promote environmental sustainability and conservation. As a renegade Chinese province, Taiwan may face challenges in implementing comprehensive environmental policies. However, as an independent country, Taiwan would have the ability to pursue its own environmental agenda and collaborate with other countries on global sustainability initiatives.

In conclusion, the implications and potential consequences of Taiwan's political status are vast and varied. Whether Taiwan remains a renegade Chinese province or becomes an independent country will shape its political, economic, social, and cultural future, as well as its relations with the international community. It is crucial for diplomats, economists, strategists, educators, historians, and the public to consider these factors when contemplating the future of Taiwan.

Economic Future of Taiwan: Opportunities and Challenges for a Renegade Chinese Province or an Independent Country

As Taiwan continues to navigate its complex political status, the economic future of the island holds both opportunities and challenges. This subchapter explores the potential pathways for Taiwan as a renegade Chinese province or an independent country, shedding light on the implications for its economy.

One of the key opportunities for Taiwan lies in its thriving technology sector. The island has long been known for its innovative prowess, with companies like TSMC leading the global semiconductor industry. As a renegade Chinese province or an independent country, Taiwan can leverage its technological advancements to attract foreign investment and foster partnerships with other nations. This could further strengthen its position as a regional hub for research and development, spurring economic growth and job creation.

However, Taiwan also faces challenges in maintaining its economic stability amidst political uncertainty. Its relationship with China, its largest trading partner, remains a delicate balance. As a renegade Chinese province, Taiwan may face economic isolation, with China imposing restrictions on trade and investment. On the other hand, if Taiwan were to become an independent country, it could face diplomatic and economic pressure from Beijing. Navigating these challenges will require strategic economic policies and diversification of trade partnerships to reduce dependence on any single market.

Another aspect to consider is the potential impact of Taiwan's political status on its efforts to promote environmental sustainability. As a renegade Chinese province or an independent country, Taiwan can develop and implement its own environmentally friendly policies without being constrained by the priorities of a larger entity. This could enhance its reputation as a responsible global citizen and attract investments in renewable energy and green technologies.

Furthermore, Taiwan's cultural identity plays a crucial role in shaping its economic future. As a renegade Chinese province, Taiwan must balance the preservation and promotion of its unique Taiwanese culture while also navigating its ties to a larger Chinese identity. This delicate balance can be an opportunity for Taiwan to develop its cultural industries, such as film, music, and tourism, attracting international attention and boosting economic growth.

In conclusion, the economic future of Taiwan as a renegade Chinese province or an independent country presents both opportunities and challenges. Leveraging its technological advancements, diversifying trade partnerships, and promoting environmental sustainability can help Taiwan thrive economically. However, it must navigate the complex dynamics of its relationship with China and preserve its cultural identity to ensure a prosperous future. By addressing these issues, Taiwan can position itself as a dynamic and resilient player in the global economy.

Economic developments in Taiwan as a renegade Chinese province

Taiwan's political status as a renegade Chinese province has had a significant impact on its economic development. Despite the challenges it faces in terms of diplomatic recognition and international relations, Taiwan has managed to establish itself as a prosperous and dynamic economy.

One of the key factors contributing to Taiwan's economic success is its commitment to innovation and technological advancements. The island nation has emerged as a global leader in the fields of electronics, semiconductors, and information technology. Taiwanese companies such as TSMC, Foxconn, and HTC are known worldwide for their cutting-edge products and have played a crucial role in driving Taiwan's economic growth.

Furthermore, Taiwan's status as a renegade Chinese province has also allowed it to forge strong economic ties with other countries. In the absence of formal diplomatic recognition, Taiwan has been able to establish trade partnerships and economic cooperation with a wide range of nations. This has enabled the island to diversify its export markets and reduce its dependence on mainland China. Taiwan's economic integration with Southeast Asia, the United States, and Europe has been instrumental in sustaining its economic growth.

Despite its economic achievements, Taiwan continues to face challenges as a renegade Chinese province. The lack of formal diplomatic recognition limits its access to international organizations and trade agreements. This hinders the island's ability to fully leverage its economic potential and participate in global decision-making processes.

Moreover, Taiwan's political status also has implications for its national security and defense strategies. As a renegade Chinese province, Taiwan faces constant military threats and pressure from mainland China. This necessitates significant investment in defense capabilities, which diverts resources that could otherwise be used for economic development.

In conclusion, Taiwan's economic development as a renegade Chinese province has been remarkable, driven by its commitment to innovation and technological advancements. However, the island faces challenges in terms of diplomatic recognition and national security. As Taiwan continues to navigate its political status, it must find ways to sustain its economic growth while addressing these challenges. International cooperation and support from the global community will be crucial in ensuring Taiwan's continued economic success as a renegade Chinese province.

Economic potential and challenges of an independent Taiwan

Introduction:

The economic potential and challenges of an independent Taiwan are crucial aspects to consider when discussing the future political status of the country. This subchapter aims to explore the opportunities and obstacles that Taiwan may encounter as a renegade Chinese province or an independent country. By analyzing its economic landscape, this section will provide insights for diplomats, economists, strategists, educators, historians, and the general public.

Economic Potential:

Taiwan has long been recognized as one of Asia's leading economies, with a highly skilled workforce and robust industrial base. In the event of independence, Taiwan would have the freedom to develop its economic policies, establish trade agreements, and expand its global market presence. With a focus on innovation and technology, Taiwan could further strengthen its position as a key player in the global supply chain. Additionally, an independent Taiwan might attract foreign investment, fueling economic growth and job creation.

Challenges:

Despite its economic strength, Taiwan faces several challenges as a renegade Chinese province or an independent country. One of the main obstacles is the potential disruption in trade relations with China, which is Taiwan's largest trading partner. The risk of economic retaliation from China might negatively impact Taiwan's export-oriented economy. Moreover, Taiwan's small size and limited natural resources pose challenges for long-term sustainability and self-sufficiency.

Opportunities for Economic Cooperation:

As an independent country, Taiwan could seek economic cooperation and trade partnerships with other nations. Strengthening ties with countries in Southeast Asia, the United States, and Europe would diversify Taiwan's export markets and reduce its dependence on China.

Furthermore, Taiwan's expertise in sectors like semiconductors, renewable energy, and biotechnology could foster international collaborations, attracting investment and fostering technological advancements.

Conclusion:

The economic potential of an independent Taiwan is significant, given its established industrial base, skilled workforce, and technological prowess. However, challenges such as trade disruptions with China and limited resources need to be addressed. By pursuing economic cooperation with other countries, diversifying export markets, and emphasizing technological advancements, Taiwan can overcome these challenges and position itself as a thriving independent nation. The opportunities for economic growth are vast, and with careful planning and strategic partnerships, Taiwan has the potential to become an economic powerhouse in the region while preserving its cultural identity and promoting environmental sustainability.

Trade relations and partnerships with other countries

Trade relations and partnerships with other countries play a crucial role in determining the future of Taiwan, whether it remains a renegade Chinese province or becomes an independent country. The economic potential and challenges faced by Taiwan in both scenarios are of great interest to diplomats, economists, strategists, educators, historians, and the general public.

As a renegade Chinese province, Taiwan's trade relations are heavily influenced by its political status. Many countries, especially those with diplomatic ties to China, are hesitant to engage in formal trade agreements with Taiwan due to fear of upsetting Beijing. However, Taiwan has managed to develop robust informal trade partnerships with numerous countries, particularly in Southeast Asia and the United

States. These partnerships have allowed Taiwan to maintain a strong export-oriented economy, with a focus on high-tech industries such as electronics and semiconductors.

If Taiwan were to become an independent country, it would have the opportunity to negotiate formal trade agreements on its own terms. This could open up new markets and diversify Taiwan's trade partners, reducing its dependence on China. With its advanced technology and skilled workforce, Taiwan has the potential to become a key player in global trade, attracting foreign investments and fostering economic growth.

However, Taiwan's quest for independence may also bring challenges in terms of trade relations. China, as a global economic powerhouse, could use its influence to pressure other countries into severing ties with Taiwan. This could potentially lead to trade restrictions and economic isolation. Therefore, Taiwan must carefully navigate its path towards independence, ensuring that it maintains strong diplomatic relationships and builds strategic partnerships to mitigate any negative repercussions.

To secure its economic future, Taiwan must also focus on technological advancements and environmental sustainability. Investing in research and development, innovation, and green technologies will not only strengthen Taiwan's competitiveness but also demonstrate its commitment to global environmental goals.

In conclusion, the trade relations and partnerships of Taiwan are deeply intertwined with its political status. Whether it remains a renegade Chinese province or becomes an independent country, Taiwan's economic future will be shaped by its ability to maintain existing trade relationships, forge new partnerships, embrace technological advancements, and promote environmental sustainability. Diplomats, economists, strategists, educators, historians, and the public must closely monitor and evaluate these factors to determine the best path forward for Taiwan's political and economic development.

Market access and economic integration considerations

As Taiwan grapples with the question of its political status, one crucial aspect that cannot be overlooked is the impact it will have on market access and economic integration. Regardless of whether Taiwan remains a renegade Chinese province or becomes an independent country, the decisions made in this regard will have far-reaching consequences for diplomats, economists, strategists, educators, historians, and the general public.

Currently, Taiwan enjoys a unique position in the global economy. It is a major player in various industries, including electronics, manufacturing, and technology. Its economic success can be attributed to its open market policies, investment-friendly environment, and strong emphasis on innovation. However, its political status poses challenges to its market access and economic integration.

If Taiwan were to remain a renegade Chinese province, it would continue to face obstacles in terms of international trade and investment. Its economic ties would be largely limited to mainland China, as many countries maintain diplomatic relations with Beijing and adhere to the "One China" policy. This would restrict Taiwan's ability to diversify its markets and increase its global economic engagement.

On the other hand, if Taiwan were to become an independent country, it would have the opportunity to establish its own trade agreements and economic partnerships with countries around the world. This would enable Taiwan to pursue a more independent economic agenda, expanding its market access and exploring new avenues for growth. However, it would also face the challenge of navigating complex international relations and competing with other established economies.

Another consideration is the potential impact on cross-strait economic integration. Currently, Taiwan and mainland China have developed deep economic ties, with many Taiwanese businesses investing heavily in China. If Taiwan were to become independent, the integration of mainland Chinese and Taiwanese societies would need to be carefully managed to avoid disruption to both economies.

Furthermore, the question of market access and economic integration also intersects with other important issues such as human rights, democracy, and environmental sustainability. Taiwan's political status will undoubtedly influence its ability to promote and protect these values, which in turn can impact its economic relationships with other countries.

In conclusion, the question of Taiwan's political status is intimately tied to considerations of market access and economic integration. The decision to remain a renegade Chinese province or become an independent country will have profound implications for Taiwan's economy and its ability to engage with the global market. Diplomats, economists, strategists, educators, historians, and the public must carefully weigh the opportunities and challenges associated with each path to ensure the long-term economic prosperity and stability of Taiwan.

International Relations: The Impact of Taiwan's Political Status on its Diplomatic Relations with Other Countries

The political status of Taiwan has long been a contentious issue, with debates focusing on whether it should remain a renegade Chinese province or become an independent country. This subchapter examines the impact of Taiwan's political status on its diplomatic relations with other countries, exploring the challenges and opportunities it presents.

Taiwan's political status has significant implications for its international relations. As a renegade Chinese province, Taiwan faces diplomatic isolation, with many countries adhering to the One China policy and refusing to establish formal diplomatic ties. This limits Taiwan's ability to engage in international organizations and participate fully in global affairs. However, as an independent country, Taiwan would have the opportunity to establish formal diplomatic relations and expand its international presence.

The economic future of Taiwan is closely intertwined with its political status. As a renegade Chinese province, Taiwan faces economic challenges, with limited access to global markets and restrictions on trade. However, as an independent country, Taiwan could pursue economic opportunities more freely and establish trade partnerships with other nations, leading to increased prosperity.

The security concerns of Taiwan are also influenced by its political status. As a renegade Chinese province, Taiwan faces the threat of military aggression from China. However, as an independent country, Taiwan could develop its national security and defense strategies independently, ensuring the safety and sovereignty of its people.

Cultural identity is another aspect impacted by Taiwan's political status. As a renegade Chinese province, Taiwan faces challenges in preserving and promoting its unique Taiwanese culture in the face of pressure to assimilate into Chinese culture. However, as an independent country, Taiwan would have the freedom to celebrate and preserve its cultural heritage.

The progress and challenges of human rights and democracy in Taiwan are also affected by its political status. As a renegade Chinese province, Taiwan faces ongoing challenges in promoting and protecting human rights and democracy, given the influence of the Chinese government. However, as an independent country, Taiwan could further advance human rights and democracy, becoming a beacon of freedom in East Asia.

In terms of economic cooperation, Taiwan's political status plays a crucial role. As a renegade Chinese province, Taiwan faces limitations in establishing economic partnerships with other countries. However, as an independent country, Taiwan could forge economic cooperation and trade partnerships, fostering growth and development.

Technological advancements also have a significant impact on Taiwan's future. As a renegade Chinese province, Taiwan faces restrictions in accessing global technological advancements. However, as an independent country, Taiwan could actively pursue technological innovation and play a leading role in shaping the future of technology.

Lastly, Taiwan's political status affects its efforts to promote environmental sustainability and conservation. As a renegade Chinese province, Taiwan faces challenges in implementing effective environmental policies due to limited international cooperation. However, as an independent country, Taiwan could take a more proactive approach towards environmental sustainability, collaborating with other nations and implementing comprehensive conservation strategies.

In conclusion, Taiwan's political status has far-reaching implications for its diplomatic relations with other countries. As a renegade Chinese province, Taiwan faces numerous challenges in terms of international recognition, economic cooperation, and cultural preservation. However, as an independent country, Taiwan would have the opportunity to strengthen its international presence, pursue economic opportunities, and safeguard its cultural identity. The impact of Taiwan's political status on various aspects such as security, human rights, technology, and environmental sustainability cannot be overlooked. It is essential to analyze and understand these complexities to envision the future of Taiwan and its role in the global community.

Taiwan's current diplomatic status

As a small island nation located off the southeastern coast of China, Taiwan's diplomatic status has long been a subject of debate and contention. Currently, Taiwan is recognized by only a handful of countries, with the majority of the international community adhering to the "One China" policy, which recognizes the People's Republic of China (PRC) as the only legitimate government of China. This has resulted in Taiwan being relegated to the status of a renegade Chinese province, rather than being recognized as an independent country.

The political status of Taiwan has far-reaching implications for various aspects of its society and future. Diplomats, economists, strategists, educators, historians, and the general public all have a vested interest in understanding the implications of Taiwan's current diplomatic status.

One of the key areas affected by Taiwan's political status is its international relations. Due to its lack of formal diplomatic recognition, Taiwan faces challenges in establishing and maintaining diplomatic relations with other countries. This has a significant impact on Taiwan's ability to engage in international cooperation, trade partnerships, and cultural exchanges.

Furthermore, Taiwan's political status also has implications for its national security and defense strategies. As a renegade Chinese province, Taiwan faces constant security concerns and the potential threat of military intervention by the PRC. This necessitates the development of robust defense strategies and close alliances with countries that support Taiwan's security interests.

Cultural identity is another important consideration in the context of Taiwan's political status. Despite being labeled as a renegade Chinese province, Taiwan has a distinct cultural identity that is deeply rooted in its history and traditions. The preservation and promotion of Taiwanese culture in the face of its political status pose significant challenges, but also offer opportunities for cultural exchange and global recognition.

Additionally, Taiwan's political status has implications for human rights and democracy. As a renegade Chinese province, Taiwan has made significant progress in the promotion and protection of human rights and democratic values. However, challenges persist, and the path towards further democratization is closely intertwined with Taiwan's political status.

In the economic sphere, Taiwan faces both opportunities and challenges. As a renegade Chinese province, Taiwan has limited access to international markets and trade partnerships. However, as an independent country, Taiwan has the potential to forge its own economic path and establish economic cooperation with other countries.

Technological advancements and environmental sustainability are also influenced by Taiwan's political status. As a renegade Chinese province or an independent country, Taiwan's ability to harness technology and promote environmental sustainability is closely tied to its diplomatic relations and international standing.

In conclusion, Taiwan's current diplomatic status as a renegade Chinese province has wide-ranging implications for its political, economic, social, and cultural future. The debates surrounding Taiwan's political status are complex and multifaceted, requiring careful consideration from diplomats, economists, strategists, educators, historians, and the general public. Understanding the consequences of Taiwan's political status is crucial for shaping the country's future and ensuring its continued development and prosperity.

The One China policy and its implications

The One China policy has been a central issue in the ongoing debate about Taiwan's political status. This policy asserts that there is only one China, and that Taiwan is a renegade province that should be reunified with the mainland. However, the implications of this policy are far-reaching and have significant consequences for various aspects of Taiwan's future.

From a political standpoint, the One China policy puts Taiwan in a precarious position. The question of whether it should remain a renegade Chinese province or become an independent country is a matter of intense debate. The outcome of this debate will determine Taiwan's future political trajectory and its ability to exercise self-governance.

Economically, the One China policy presents both opportunities and challenges. As a renegade Chinese province, Taiwan has been able to leverage its economic strengths to forge international trade partnerships and attract foreign investment. However, the threat of diplomatic isolation looms large, as many countries adhere to the One China policy and refuse to establish formal diplomatic relations with Taiwan.

The One China policy also has implications for Taiwan's national security and defense strategies. As a renegade Chinese province, Taiwan faces the constant risk of military aggression from the mainland. This necessitates a strong focus on defense capabilities and strategic alliances to ensure the country's security.

Culturally, the One China policy poses challenges to the preservation and promotion of Taiwanese culture. The renegade Chinese province status undermines Taiwan's distinct cultural identity, making it vulnerable to assimilation and erasure. Efforts to safeguard and promote Taiwanese culture become essential in the face of this policy.

Human rights and democracy are also impacted by the One China policy. Taiwan has made significant progress in these areas, but the renegade Chinese province status poses challenges to the further development of human rights and democracy. Struggles for autonomy and self-determination are inherent in this complex political situation.

In terms of social integration, the event of Taiwan becoming an independent country would necessitate the integration of mainland Chinese and Taiwanese societies. This process would require delicate negotiations and efforts to bridge cultural, social, and political differences.

Economically, Taiwan has the potential to forge economic cooperation and trade partnerships with other countries as both a renegade Chinese province and an independent country. However, the One China policy adds an additional layer of complexity to these negotiations and requires careful navigation.

Technological advancements play a crucial role in shaping Taiwan's future, regardless of its political status. The country's technological prowess can provide a foundation for economic growth and innovation, and can also contribute to its international standing.

Finally, the One China policy has implications for Taiwan's efforts to promote environmental sustainability and conservation. As a renegade Chinese province, Taiwan faces challenges in coordinating efforts with other countries and accessing international resources and expertise in this area.

In conclusion, the One China policy has far-reaching implications for Taiwan's political, economic, cultural, and social future. The ongoing debate about whether it should remain a renegade Chinese province or become an independent country has significant consequences for various aspects of Taiwanese society. Understanding these implications is crucial for diplomats, economists, strategists, educators, historians, and the general public alike.

Diplomatic challenges and opportunities for Taiwan

In the complex global arena, Taiwan faces numerous diplomatic challenges and opportunities, stemming from its unique political status. As a renegade Chinese province or a potential independent country, Taiwan's foreign relations are subject to constant scrutiny and negotiation. Understanding these dynamics is crucial for diplomats, economists, strategists, educators, historians, and the public.

Taiwan's political status directly impacts its diplomatic relations with other countries. Currently, only a handful of nations officially recognize Taiwan as a sovereign state due to pressure from China. This status quo limits Taiwan's participation in international organizations and hampers its ability to engage in meaningful diplomatic exchanges. However, recent developments have shown that some countries are willing to foster closer ties with Taiwan, recognizing its economic prowess and democratic values. Diplomats and strategists must carefully navigate this delicate balance, capitalizing on opportunities to strengthen Taiwan's international standing while mitigating potential backlash from China.

The economic future of Taiwan also hinges on its political status. As a renegade Chinese province, Taiwan faces challenges in securing and expanding trade partnerships. However, as an independent country, it can pursue economic cooperation more freely, fostering innovation, attracting investments, and diversifying its economic base. Economists and strategists must explore avenues to maximize Taiwan's economic potential, leveraging its strengths in technology, manufacturing, and services sectors, and forging strategic partnerships with like-minded nations.

Taiwan's national security and defense strategies are intricately tied to its political status. As a renegade Chinese province, Taiwan faces constant military threats and must invest heavily in defense capabilities. However, as an independent country, it can shape its defense strategies more autonomously, cooperating with international partners to enhance its security. Strategists and defense experts must assess the evolving geopolitical landscape and design comprehensive security frameworks to safeguard Taiwan's sovereignty.

Cultural identity is another crucial aspect impacted by Taiwan's political status. As a renegade Chinese province, Taiwan faces challenges in preserving and promoting its distinct Taiwanese culture. Efforts must be made to protect cultural heritage, foster cultural exchanges, and raise international awareness about Taiwan's unique identity. Educators, historians, and cultural enthusiasts must collaborate to ensure the preservation of Taiwanese culture amidst the pressures of assimilation.

The progress and challenges of human rights and democracy in Taiwan are also influenced by its political status. As a renegade Chinese province, Taiwan faces limitations on its democratic development, with potential infringements on human rights. However, as an independent country, Taiwan can further strengthen its democratic institutions and advocate for human rights at the international level. Scholars, activists, and policymakers must work together to consolidate Taiwan's democratic gains and address any lingering challenges.

In the event of Taiwan becoming an independent country, the integration of mainland Chinese and Taiwanese societies would be a significant task. Diplomats, educators, and social integration experts must facilitate dialogue, build trust, and promote mutual understanding to ensure a peaceful and harmonious transition.

Taiwan's political status also affects its potential for economic cooperation and trade partnerships. As a renegade Chinese province,

Taiwan faces limitations in forging international economic ties. However, as an independent country, it can establish mutually beneficial trade agreements, leverage its technological advancements, and actively participate in regional economic integration efforts. Economists, diplomats, and trade experts must explore opportunities for economic cooperation, capitalizing on Taiwan's strengths and building lasting partnerships.

Technological advancements play a pivotal role in shaping Taiwan's future, regardless of its political status. As a renegade Chinese province or an independent country, Taiwan must continue to invest in research and development, foster innovation, and embrace emerging technologies. Technologists, policymakers, and economists must collaborate to ensure Taiwan's technological competitiveness and its ability to navigate the global digital landscape.

Lastly, Taiwan's political status has implications for its environmental sustainability efforts. As a renegade Chinese province or an independent country, Taiwan must prioritize environmental conservation, adopt sustainable practices, and participate in global climate initiatives. Policymakers, environmentalists, and economists must work together to mitigate the potential impact of Taiwan's political status on its environmental goals.

In conclusion, the diplomatic challenges and opportunities for Taiwan are vast and multifaceted. Addressing these issues requires close collaboration between diplomats, economists, strategists, educators, historians, and the public. By understanding the nuances of Taiwan's political status, stakeholders can chart a path that maximizes opportunities, safeguards Taiwan's interests, and ensures a prosperous and sustainable future for the island nation.

Case studies of countries' diplomatic relations with Taiwan

Taiwan's political status as a renegade Chinese province has had a significant impact on its diplomatic relations with other countries. In this subchapter, we will examine case studies of several countries and their unique approaches in establishing and maintaining diplomatic ties with Taiwan.

One intriguing case study is the United States. Despite not officially recognizing Taiwan as a sovereign nation, the US has maintained strong unofficial relations with the island. This relationship is rooted in the Taiwan Relations Act, which ensures the continuation of economic, cultural, and security cooperation between the two entities. The US's support for Taiwan is seen as a cornerstone of its Indo-Pacific strategy and a counterbalance to China's growing influence in the region.

Another case study is Japan, which maintains a similar unofficial relationship with Taiwan. Japan has a long history of cultural and economic exchanges with Taiwan, and in recent years, has increased its support for Taiwan's participation in international organizations. However, Japan treads carefully to avoid antagonizing China, as it seeks to balance its economic interests with maintaining regional stability.

In contrast, China's diplomatic efforts have been focused on isolating Taiwan on the international stage. It pressures countries to sever ties with Taiwan in favor of recognizing the One-China policy. This has led to a shrinking number of countries that officially recognize Taiwan, with only a handful of small nations maintaining formal diplomatic relations.

However, there have been some notable exceptions. For example, the Holy See, the sovereign entity of Vatican City, maintains diplomatic relations with Taiwan despite its lack of recognition from China. This unique relationship is based on shared values and religious ties, as well as the Vatican's support for Taiwan's human rights and democracy.

These case studies highlight the complexities and challenges surrounding Taiwan's diplomatic relations. As Taiwan's political status remains in question, countries must carefully navigate their relationships with both Taiwan and China. The decisions made by these countries have far-reaching implications for Taiwan's international standing and its ability to engage in global affairs.

In conclusion, understanding the case studies of countries' diplomatic relations with Taiwan provides valuable insights into the complex nature of Taiwan's political status. These case studies reveal the varying approaches taken by different countries and shed light on the opportunities and challenges faced by Taiwan in its quest for international recognition. As diplomats, economists, strategists, educators, historians, and the public, it is crucial to examine and analyze these case studies to gain a comprehensive understanding of Taiwan's diplomatic landscape.

Security Concerns: How Taiwan's Political Status Affects its National Security and Defense Strategies

Introduction:

Taiwan's political status as a renegade Chinese province or an independent country has significant implications for its national security and defense strategies. This subchapter examines the security concerns that arise from Taiwan's unresolved political status, and how it impacts the island's defense policies. Understanding these challenges is crucial for diplomats, economists, strategists, educators, historians, and the public as they seek to comprehend the complexities surrounding Taiwan's future.

The strategic importance of Taiwan:

Taiwan's location in the heart of East Asia makes it strategically vital, with geopolitical implications that extend beyond its borders. As a renegade Chinese province, Taiwan faces continuous security threats from the mainland, including the possibility of a military invasion. However, as an independent country, Taiwan would need to navigate the delicate balance of maintaining regional stability while safeguarding its sovereignty.

The impact of political status on defense strategies:

Taiwan's political status significantly impacts its defense strategies. As a renegade Chinese province, Taiwan relies on the United States for military support and defense cooperation. However, this reliance creates a certain level of vulnerability, as any change in the international dynamics could potentially limit or diminish U.S. support. On the other hand, as an independent country, Taiwan would need to develop a self-sufficient defense capability to ensure its security. This would require significant investment in military modernization and technology, as well as the cultivation of strong alliances with like-minded nations.

The role of diplomacy:

Taiwan's political status also influences its diplomatic relations, which directly impact its security. As a renegade Chinese province, Taiwan faces significant challenges in maintaining formal diplomatic recognition from other countries due to pressure from China. This limits its ability to build strong alliances and partnerships that could enhance its security posture. Conversely, if Taiwan were to become an independent country, it could pursue a more proactive foreign policy, expanding its diplomatic reach and forging alliances based on shared security interests.

Conclusion:

The unresolved political status of Taiwan poses significant security concerns for the island. Whether it remains a renegade Chinese province or becomes an independent country, Taiwan must address these challenges to ensure its national security and defense strategies are robust and effective. The international community, including diplomats, economists, strategists, educators, historians, and the general public, must carefully consider these security concerns as they engage in discussions about Taiwan's future. Finding a sustainable and secure path forward for Taiwan is crucial not only for the island but also for regional stability and the broader international order.

Taiwan's defense capabilities and strategies

Taiwan's defense capabilities and strategies play a crucial role in shaping its future as a renegade Chinese province or an independent country. With its unique political status and complex relations with China, Taiwan faces numerous security concerns that require careful consideration and planning.

Despite its smaller size and population, Taiwan has invested heavily in building a strong defense force to ensure its sovereignty and protect its people. The country has developed advanced military technologies, including indigenous missile systems, submarines, and fighter jets. Moreover, Taiwan has established a robust defense industry that contributes to its self-sufficiency and enhances its defense capabilities.

Taiwan's defense strategies focus on maintaining a credible deterrent against potential aggression from China while seeking peaceful resolution of conflicts. The country adopts a multi-faceted approach that includes a combination of conventional and asymmetric warfare tactics. Taiwan's military emphasizes the importance of joint operations, intelligence gathering, and cyber defense to counter potential threats effectively.

In recent years, Taiwan has also sought to enhance its international defense cooperation to strengthen its security network. The country has engaged in military exchanges, joint exercises, and arms procurement with key allies, such as the United States and Japan. These partnerships not only provide Taiwan with advanced military technologies but also serve as a deterrent against potential aggression.

However, Taiwan's defense capabilities and strategies face challenges due to its renegade Chinese province status. China's increasing military modernization and assertive behavior pose significant threats to Taiwan's security. The constant military maneuvers and airspace violations by China near Taiwan's borders create an environment of uncertainty and instability.

To address these challenges, Taiwan needs to continuously upgrade its defense capabilities and invest in advanced technologies. Additionally, the country must enhance its intelligence gathering and surveillance capabilities to effectively monitor potential threats. Strengthening regional and international defense cooperation is also crucial to deter potential aggression and ensure Taiwan's security.

In conclusion, Taiwan's defense capabilities and strategies are vital for its future as a renegade Chinese province or an independent country. The country's investment in advanced military technologies, robust defense industry, and international defense cooperation contribute to its security and sovereignty. However, challenges from China's military modernization and assertiveness require continuous efforts to enhance defense capabilities and strengthen security networks. Only through a comprehensive and proactive defense strategy can Taiwan safeguard its political status and ensure a peaceful and secure future.

External threats and regional security dynamics

In the ever-changing landscape of international politics, Taiwan faces numerous external threats and regional security dynamics that have a direct impact on its political status as a renegade Chinese province or an independent country. This subchapter aims to shed light on the complexities and challenges that Taiwan encounters in terms of its security concerns and the broader dynamics of the region.

When discussing external threats, it is impossible to ignore the looming presence of China. With its growing economic and military power, China seeks to assert its authority over Taiwan and considers it an integral part of its territory. This has resulted in increased military provocations, such as airspace violations and naval exercises near Taiwan's shores. These actions pose a direct threat to Taiwan's national security and require a robust defense strategy to ensure its sovereignty.

Furthermore, Taiwan's political status has a significant impact on its diplomatic relations with other countries. China's influence and pressure tactics have resulted in many countries severing official ties with Taiwan in favor of recognizing China. This limits Taiwan's ability to participate fully in international organizations and hampers its diplomatic efforts to secure support for its independent status. As a result, Taiwan often finds itself isolated on the global stage, making it vulnerable to external threats.

The regional security dynamics in East Asia also play a crucial role in shaping Taiwan's political status. The delicate balance of power between China, the United States, and other regional players creates a complex web of alliances and strategic interests. Any escalation of tensions in the region, such as conflicts in the Korean Peninsula or the South China Sea, directly impacts Taiwan's security and its ability to maintain its renegade Chinese province status or pursue independence.

In conclusion, Taiwan's political status as a renegade Chinese province or an independent country is intricately linked to external threats and regional security dynamics. China's assertiveness, diplomatic isolation, and the ever-changing regional landscape pose significant challenges to Taiwan's national security and defense strategies. Understanding and addressing these issues is crucial for diplomats, economists, strategists, educators, historians, and the general public to comprehend the complexities of Taiwan's political future and its impact on regional stability.

The role of alliances and partnerships in Taiwan's security

The role of alliances and partnerships plays a crucial role in ensuring Taiwan's security in the face of its renegade Chinese province status. Taiwan, as a small island nation, faces numerous security challenges due to its proximity to mainland China and its complex political status. In order to navigate these challenges, Taiwan has actively sought alliances and partnerships with like-minded nations.

One of the key alliances that Taiwan has cultivated is with the United States. The U.S. has been a long-standing ally of Taiwan and has played a significant role in ensuring its security. Through the Taiwan Relations Act, the U.S. has committed to providing Taiwan with defensive weapons and has supported its participation in international organizations. This alliance not only serves as a deterrent to potential aggressors but also enhances Taiwan's ability to defend itself.

In addition to the United States, Taiwan has also sought partnerships with other countries and regional organizations. These partnerships serve multiple purposes, including promoting economic cooperation, enhancing diplomatic relations, and sharing intelligence and security expertise. For instance, Taiwan has developed close ties with Japan, Australia, and European countries, which have contributed to its economic development and security.

Furthermore, Taiwan's security is not solely dependent on military alliances. The island has also actively engaged in regional security forums and initiatives, such as the ASEAN Regional Forum and the Pacific Islands Forum. Through these platforms, Taiwan has been able to build relationships with neighboring countries and contribute to regional security cooperation.

However, Taiwan's efforts to form alliances and partnerships are not without challenges. One of the main obstacles is China's opposition to any country establishing official diplomatic relations with Taiwan. China considers Taiwan as part of its territory and has used its economic and political influence to discourage countries from recognizing or supporting Taiwan. This poses a significant challenge for Taiwan's security, as it limits its ability to form formal alliances with many nations.

In conclusion, alliances and partnerships are vital for Taiwan's security in the face of its renegade Chinese province status. These alliances provide Taiwan with diplomatic support, economic opportunities, and access to security expertise. While challenges exist, Taiwan's proactive engagement with like-minded nations and regional organizations enhances its security and contributes to regional stability.

Potential scenarios and challenges for Taiwan's security as a renegade Chinese province or an independent country

The political status of Taiwan has long been a contentious issue, with debates focusing on whether it should remain a renegade Chinese province or become an independent country. This subchapter explores the potential scenarios and challenges for Taiwan's security under each of these options.

As a renegade Chinese province, Taiwan faces significant security challenges. China's assertiveness in the region poses a threat to Taiwan's territorial integrity, as demonstrated by its increasing military presence and frequent military exercises near the Taiwan Strait. In this scenario, Taiwan must rely on its own military capabilities to deter potential aggression and maintain stability in the region. Strengthening defense strategies and building alliances with like-minded countries would be crucial to ensure Taiwan's security.

On the other hand, if Taiwan were to become an independent country, it would face a different set of security challenges. The most immediate concern would be China's response to such a move. Beijing has consistently maintained that it would use force to prevent Taiwan from declaring independence. This raises questions about the potential for military conflict and the impact it would have on regional stability. Taiwan would need to invest heavily in its defense capabilities and seek support from the international community to deter China's aggression.

In addition to external security challenges, Taiwan would also need to address internal security concerns. The integration of mainland Chinese and Taiwanese societies, as well as the preservation of Taiwanese culture, would be key issues to navigate. Ensuring social cohesion and maintaining stability in the face of potential political and cultural divisions would be essential.

Furthermore, Taiwan's political status would have implications for its diplomatic relations with other countries. As a renegade Chinese province, Taiwan faces diplomatic isolation, with only a handful of countries recognizing its sovereignty. However, as an independent country, Taiwan would have the opportunity to expand its diplomatic ties and forge new economic partnerships. This would require careful navigation of the complex web of international relations and an understanding of the potential consequences for regional stability.

Overall, regardless of whether Taiwan remains a renegade Chinese province or becomes an independent country, security concerns will persist. The future of Taiwan's security hinges on its ability to adapt to changing geopolitical dynamics, strengthen its defense capabilities, and build strong alliances with like-minded countries. It is essential for diplomats, economists, strategists, educators, historians, and the public to understand these potential scenarios and challenges and work towards a secure future for Taiwan.

Cultural Identity: The Preservation and Promotion of Taiwanese Culture in the Face of its Renegade Chinese Province Status

Taiwan's unique cultural identity has long been shaped by its complex history and its status as a renegade Chinese province. Despite facing challenges and pressure from China, Taiwan has successfully preserved and promoted its rich cultural heritage, making it an important aspect of its national identity.

Taiwanese culture is a vibrant fusion of indigenous traditions, Chinese heritage, and influences from various immigrant communities. From its traditional arts and crafts, such as calligraphy, painting, and pottery, to its renowned culinary scene, Taiwan's cultural diversity is a testament to its resilience and ability to withstand external forces.

In the face of its renegade Chinese province status, Taiwan has made significant efforts to preserve and promote its cultural heritage. The government has established institutions and organizations dedicated to cultural preservation, such as the Ministry of Culture and the National Museum of Taiwan. These institutions work tirelessly to document, protect, and showcase Taiwan's unique cultural assets.

Moreover, Taiwan actively participates in international cultural exchanges, showcasing its cultural treasures to the world. Through events like the annual Taipei Lantern Festival, the Taiwan International Festival of Arts, and the Golden Melody Awards, Taiwan celebrates its cultural diversity and fosters dialogue with other nations.

Education also plays a crucial role in preserving Taiwanese culture. Schools and universities incorporate cultural studies into their curriculum, ensuring that younger generations understand and appreciate their cultural roots. In addition, the government supports initiatives that promote cultural awareness and understanding among the public, such as heritage tours, cultural festivals, and exhibitions.

Taiwan's cultural preservation efforts not only serve to strengthen its national identity but also contribute to its soft power on the international stage. By showcasing its unique cultural heritage, Taiwan attracts tourists, enhances its diplomatic relations, and fosters cultural exchanges with other countries.

In conclusion, despite its renegade Chinese province status, Taiwan has successfully preserved and promoted its cultural identity. Through government support, educational initiatives, and international cultural exchanges, Taiwan continues to showcase its rich heritage to the world. As Taiwan navigates its future political status, the preservation and promotion of its cultural identity will remain a crucial aspect of its national development.

Taiwanese cultural heritage and identity

Taiwan's rich cultural heritage and identity have played a significant role in shaping the island's history and its people's sense of belonging. Despite its renegade Chinese province status, Taiwan has managed to preserve and promote its unique cultural traditions, allowing its citizens to maintain a distinct Taiwanese identity.

Taiwanese culture is a fusion of indigenous, Chinese, and Japanese influences, creating a diverse and vibrant tapestry that reflects the island's complex history. From its traditional arts, such as calligraphy, painting, and puppetry, to its culinary delights, such as bubble tea and night market snacks, Taiwanese culture has captivated people from all over the world.

One of the challenges faced by Taiwan in preserving its cultural heritage is the threat of assimilation under the renegade Chinese province status. The Chinese government has made efforts to undermine Taiwan's cultural identity by promoting a homogenized "Chinese" culture and discouraging the recognition of Taiwan's distinct heritage. However, the Taiwanese people have firmly resisted these attempts, cherishing their unique traditions and passing them down through generations.

In recent years, Taiwan has made significant strides in promoting its cultural heritage both domestically and internationally. The government has implemented policies to safeguard and revitalize traditional arts, support local artisans, and establish cultural centers and museums. These initiatives have not only preserved Taiwanese culture but have also boosted tourism and contributed to the island's economy.

Furthermore, the international community has recognized Taiwan's cultural contributions, allowing the island to participate in various cultural events and exchange programs. Taiwanese films, music, and literature have gained global recognition, showcasing the island's creative talents and fostering a sense of pride among Taiwanese people.

The preservation and promotion of Taiwanese culture are not only essential for maintaining Taiwan's distinct identity but also for fostering social cohesion and inclusivity. Embracing diversity and celebrating cultural heritage can bridge the divide between mainland Chinese and Taiwanese societies, fostering mutual understanding and dialogue.

In conclusion, Taiwanese cultural heritage and identity are integral to the island's history, society, and future. Despite the challenges posed by its renegade Chinese province status, Taiwan has managed to preserve and promote its unique traditions, allowing its citizens to maintain a strong sense of Taiwanese identity. By continuing to support cultural preservation efforts and promoting international exchanges, Taiwan can ensure that its cultural heritage thrives in the face of political complexities.

Challenges to cultural preservation under renegade Chinese province status

As the political status of Taiwan remains in question, one of the significant challenges it faces is the preservation of its unique cultural identity. With the label of a renegade Chinese province, Taiwan's cultural heritage faces threats from assimilation and erasure. This subchapter explores the obstacles that Taiwan encounters in its pursuit of cultural preservation and promotion.

Taiwan boasts a rich and diverse cultural heritage, drawing influences from its indigenous people, Chinese immigrants, and Japanese colonization. However, under the renegade Chinese province status, Taiwan's cultural identity faces the risk of being overshadowed by the dominant Chinese culture. The Chinese government's claim over Taiwan and its efforts to assert authority often undermine the preservation of local traditions, languages, and customs.

One of the challenges to cultural preservation lies in education. The Chinese government's influence on the curriculum of Taiwanese schools promotes a Chinese-centric view, neglecting the unique history and culture of Taiwan. This hinders the younger generation's understanding and appreciation of their own heritage, leading to a potential loss of cultural identity.

Another challenge is the commercialization of culture. As Taiwan seeks to boost its economy, there is a temptation to capitalize on cultural artifacts and traditions for tourism purposes. However, this can lead to commodification and dilution of the authentic cultural expressions, eroding their significance and authenticity.

Furthermore, the political ambiguity surrounding Taiwan's status creates difficulties in international cultural exchange and cooperation. Many countries are cautious about engaging in cultural partnerships with

Taiwan, fearing diplomatic repercussions from China. This limits Taiwan's opportunities to showcase its unique culture on the global stage and hampers efforts to preserve and promote it.

To overcome these challenges, Taiwan must adopt comprehensive strategies. It should invest in cultural education that emphasizes Taiwanese history, traditions, and languages. By fostering a sense of pride and understanding among its citizens, Taiwan can secure its cultural heritage for future generations.

Additionally, Taiwan should establish cultural preservation programs that engage local communities, artists, and scholars. Through funding and support, these initiatives can safeguard endangered cultural practices, encourage artistic innovation, and promote cultural exchanges both domestically and internationally.

Furthermore, Taiwan can leverage its technological advancements to preserve and promote its cultural heritage. Digital platforms, virtual reality, and augmented reality can be utilized to create immersive experiences, allowing people to engage with Taiwan's traditions, history, and cultural artifacts.

In conclusion, the challenges to cultural preservation under the renegade Chinese province status are significant but not insurmountable. Taiwan must prioritize the preservation of its cultural identity by investing in education, establishing preservation programs, and leveraging technology. By doing so, Taiwan can ensure the survival and promotion of its vibrant and diverse cultural heritage.

Efforts to promote and preserve Taiwanese culture

Taiwanese culture is a rich tapestry of traditions, languages, and customs that have evolved over centuries. Despite its renegade Chinese province status, Taiwan has made concerted efforts to promote and preserve its unique cultural identity. This subchapter explores the various initiatives undertaken by the government and civil society to safeguard Taiwanese culture in the face of political challenges.

The Taiwanese government has recognized the importance of cultural preservation and has implemented policies to support and promote the arts. Cultural institutions, such as the National Palace Museum and the National Taiwan Museum, have been established to showcase Taiwan's rich history and cultural heritage. These institutions play a vital role in educating both locals and international visitors about Taiwanese culture.

Furthermore, the government has invested in the preservation of traditional Taiwanese arts, including puppetry, opera, and music. The Ministry of Culture provides funding and resources to support artists and cultural organizations, ensuring that these art forms continue to thrive and evolve.

In addition to government initiatives, civil society groups have also played a significant role in promoting Taiwanese culture. Non-profit organizations, such as the Taiwan Cultural Association and the Taiwan Academy, organize cultural events, exhibitions, and workshops to raise awareness and appreciation for Taiwanese traditions.

Language is an integral part of cultural identity, and efforts have been made to protect and promote the Taiwanese language. The government has implemented policies to encourage the use of Taiwanese in schools and public institutions, recognizing it as a distinct language separate from Mandarin Chinese.

Taiwanese cuisine is another aspect of the culture that has gained international recognition. The government has supported culinary initiatives, such as food festivals and international culinary exchanges, to promote Taiwanese cuisine and enhance its global presence.

Despite the challenges posed by its political status, Taiwan continues to foster an environment that celebrates and preserves its unique cultural heritage. The efforts of the government and civil society have resulted in increased awareness and appreciation for Taiwanese culture, both domestically and internationally.

By promoting and preserving its cultural identity, Taiwan not only strengthens its sense of national pride but also enhances its soft power on the international stage. The preservation of Taiwanese culture is not only essential for the people of Taiwan but also contributes to the global tapestry of diversity and cultural understanding.

In conclusion, Taiwan's efforts to promote and preserve its culture in the face of its renegade Chinese province status have been commendable. Through government initiatives and the dedication of civil society groups, Taiwan has managed to safeguard its rich cultural heritage. The preservation of Taiwanese culture is crucial not only for the people of Taiwan but also for the global community's appreciation and understanding of diverse cultural identities.

Cultural diplomacy and international recognition

In the complex and ever-evolving landscape of international relations, cultural diplomacy plays a crucial role in shaping a nation's identity and international recognition. This subchapter delves into the importance of cultural diplomacy for Taiwan, examining how it can influence its political status as a renegade Chinese province or an independent country.

Taiwan's unique cultural heritage is a testament to its rich history and diverse identity. By preserving and promoting Taiwanese culture, Taiwan can establish itself as a distinct entity, separate from mainland China. Cultural diplomacy becomes a powerful tool in this endeavor as it allows Taiwan to showcase its vibrant arts, literature, cuisine, and traditions to the world.

For diplomats, cultural diplomacy serves as a means to foster mutual understanding and build bridges with other nations. By engaging in cultural exchanges, Taiwan can establish people-to-people connections, promote dialogue, and dispel misconceptions about its political status. This can lead to greater international recognition and support for Taiwan's aspirations to become an independent country.

Economists and strategists also have a stake in cultural diplomacy. Taiwan's cultural exports, such as music, films, and technology, have gained international acclaim. Leveraging these cultural assets, Taiwan can expand its economic opportunities and forge trade partnerships with countries that appreciate its unique cultural products. This can contribute to the growth of Taiwan's economy, regardless of its political status.

Educators and historians play a vital role in preserving and transmitting Taiwanese culture to future generations. By integrating Taiwanese history, language, and cultural practices into the education system, Taiwan can ensure the continuity of its cultural identity. This will instill a sense of pride and belonging among Taiwanese citizens and contribute to the preservation of their cultural heritage.

The public, as beneficiaries of cultural diplomacy, have the power to shape Taiwan's international recognition. By actively participating in cultural events, supporting local artists, and showcasing Taiwanese culture on social media platforms, the public can contribute to the global recognition of Taiwan as an independent country.

In conclusion, cultural diplomacy is a multifaceted tool that can significantly impact Taiwan's international recognition. By preserving and promoting its unique cultural heritage, Taiwan can establish its distinct identity and garner support for its political aspirations. Cultural diplomacy not only paves the way for stronger diplomatic relations but also drives economic growth, fosters social integration, and contributes to environmental sustainability. It is a powerful force that can shape the future of Taiwan, regardless of its political status.

Human Rights and Democracy: The Progress and Challenges of Human Rights and Democracy in Taiwan as a Renegade Chinese Province or an Independent Country

Taiwan has made significant progress in the promotion and protection of human rights and democracy, despite its complex political status as a renegade Chinese province. The island nation has been a beacon of democratic values and has consistently ranked high in global democracy indices. However, it continues to face challenges in its pursuit of human rights and democracy due to its ambiguous political status.

Under the renegade Chinese province status, Taiwan has managed to establish a robust democratic system, upholding the principles of free and fair elections, freedom of speech, and the rule of law. It has developed strong institutions that safeguard civil liberties and political rights, ensuring that its citizens enjoy a high degree of individual freedoms. The vibrant civil society and active participation of the public in political affairs are testaments to the progress made in Taiwan's democratic development.

However, Taiwan's political status poses challenges to the full realization of human rights and democracy. Its lack of international recognition limits its ability to participate fully in international human rights mechanisms and hampers its diplomatic relations with other countries. This has a direct impact on its efforts to promote human rights globally and address human rights abuses in the region.

Additionally, Taiwan faces pressure from China, which claims sovereignty over the island. China's influence has resulted in limitations on Taiwan's international participation and the suppression of its voice in global forums. This poses challenges to the protection of human rights and democracy, as Taiwan is often excluded from crucial discussions on human rights issues.

Despite these challenges, Taiwan remains committed to upholding human rights and democracy. The government continues to enact legislation and implement policies that promote equality, protect minority rights, and ensure the freedom of expression. Civil society organizations play a crucial role in monitoring human rights violations and advocating for change.

Looking ahead, Taiwan's pursuit of human rights and democracy will depend on its political status. If Taiwan were to become an independent country, it would have the opportunity to strengthen its engagement with the international community, enhance its human rights advocacy, and expand its democratic influence globally. However, even as a renegade Chinese province, Taiwan can continue to make progress by leveraging its achievements and engaging with like-minded countries and organizations that share its commitment to human rights and democracy.

In conclusion, Taiwan has made remarkable strides in the promotion and protection of human rights and democracy, despite its renegade Chinese province status. However, challenges persist, primarily due to limited international recognition and pressure from China. Taiwan's future as an independent country holds the promise of further advancing human rights and democracy on the global stage, but even as a renegade Chinese province, it can continue to make progress through strategic engagement and collaboration with the international community.

Evolution of human rights and democracy in Taiwan

Taiwan has made significant strides in the evolution of human rights and democracy, despite its ambiguous political status as a renegade Chinese province or an independent country. This subchapter aims to explore the progress and challenges faced by Taiwan in the realm of human rights and democracy, shedding light on the country's achievements and the road ahead.

Since the end of martial law in 1987, Taiwan has undergone a remarkable transformation from an authoritarian regime to a vibrant democracy. The Taiwanese people have enjoyed greater civil liberties, including freedom of speech, assembly, and the press. Political parties have flourished, and regular elections have become the norm, showcasing Taiwan's commitment to democratic principles.

Furthermore, Taiwan has taken significant steps to safeguard human rights. The government has enacted legislation to protect the rights of women, indigenous peoples, and other marginalized groups. Efforts have been made to combat human trafficking, promote gender equality, and ensure the rights of LGBTQ+ individuals.

Taiwan's commitment to human rights has also extended to the international stage. Despite its limited diplomatic recognition, Taiwan has actively participated in global human rights initiatives and international organizations. It has offered support to countries in need, providing humanitarian aid and sharing its democratic experiences.

However, Taiwan continues to face challenges in its pursuit of human rights and democracy. The country's political status remains a hindrance, as it limits its ability to fully participate in international forums and engage in bilateral relations. The threat of Chinese interference looms over Taiwan's democratic institutions, creating a delicate balancing act between autonomy and external pressures.

Moreover, the preservation and promotion of Taiwanese culture in the face of its renegade Chinese province status is another challenge. The government has implemented policies to protect and promote

Taiwanese culture and language, but the ongoing cultural assimilation from mainland China poses a threat to the distinct Taiwanese identity.

In conclusion, Taiwan's journey towards human rights and democracy has been marked by significant progress. However, the country continues to face challenges, both internally and externally, in its pursuit of these ideals. As Taiwan grapples with its political status, it must remain steadfast in its commitment to human rights and democracy, advocating for its values on the global stage and safeguarding the rights of its citizens.

Human rights challenges under renegade Chinese province status

The renegade Chinese province status of Taiwan poses significant challenges to the protection and promotion of human rights on the island. Despite significant progress in recent decades, Taiwan continues to face obstacles in ensuring the full realization of human rights for its citizens.

One of the main challenges is the limited international recognition of Taiwan's political status. As a renegade province, Taiwan is often excluded from international forums and organizations, which hinders its ability to advocate for human rights on the global stage. This lack of recognition also limits the international scrutiny and pressure that could be exerted on China to improve its human rights record, both within its borders and in relation to Taiwan.

Within Taiwan itself, the renegade province status also creates challenges for the protection of human rights. The threat of Chinese interference looms large, as Beijing has been known to exert pressure on other countries to limit their engagement with Taiwan. This can have a chilling effect on civil society organizations and individuals advocating for human rights, as they may face harassment, intimidation, or even imprisonment.

The renegade province status also affects Taiwan's ability to fully participate in international human rights mechanisms. For example, Taiwan is not a member of the United Nations, which means it cannot directly contribute to the development of international human rights standards and mechanisms. This limits its capacity to shape global norms and policies that could benefit the protection of human rights in Taiwan and beyond.

Furthermore, the renegade province status also creates challenges for the protection of specific rights, such as freedom of expression and assembly. The fear of Chinese reprisals can lead to self-censorship and a chilling effect on public discourse. In addition, the renegade province status makes it difficult for Taiwan to fully engage with international human rights organizations and access resources and expertise that could help address these challenges.

Despite these challenges, Taiwan has made significant progress in the promotion of human rights and democracy. It has implemented comprehensive legal frameworks to protect human rights, including the establishment of an independent judiciary and a vibrant civil society. Furthermore, Taiwan has taken steps to strengthen its democratic institutions and promote transparency and accountability.

In conclusion, the renegade Chinese province status of Taiwan poses significant challenges to the protection and promotion of human rights on the island. Limited international recognition, Chinese interference, and exclusion from international mechanisms all contribute to these challenges. However, Taiwan has made significant progress and remains committed to upholding human rights and democracy. Continued international support and engagement are crucial to overcoming these challenges and ensuring the full realization of human rights in Taiwan.

Democratic achievements and challenges

Taiwan's journey towards democracy has been marked by significant achievements and ongoing challenges. As a renegade Chinese province, Taiwan has made remarkable progress in establishing a robust democratic system that values human rights, freedom of expression, and the rule of law. However, the path towards full democratic consolidation remains complex and multifaceted.

One of the most significant democratic achievements in Taiwan is the peaceful transition of power through free and fair elections. Over the years, Taiwan has successfully conducted several presidential and legislative elections, demonstrating the maturity and resilience of its democratic institutions. The Taiwanese people have embraced their role as active participants in the democratic process, fostering a vibrant political culture and ensuring that their voices are heard.

Moreover, Taiwan has made remarkable strides in the protection and promotion of human rights. It has implemented comprehensive legislation to safeguard civil liberties, including freedom of speech, assembly, and religion. The establishment of an independent judiciary has further strengthened the democratic fabric of Taiwan, ensuring equal protection under the law and fostering a sense of justice among its citizens.

Despite these achievements, challenges persist. Taiwan's political status as a renegade Chinese province poses significant hurdles to its pursuit of international recognition and participation in global institutions. The Chinese government's relentless efforts to isolate Taiwan diplomatically have limited its ability to engage fully with the international community. This has not only hampered Taiwan's diplomatic relations but also hindered its economic cooperation and trade partnerships with other countries.

Taiwan's democratic journey also faces challenges in terms of social integration. The prospect of Taiwan becoming an independent country raises questions about the integration of mainland Chinese and Taiwanese societies. Bridging the cultural, social, and political gaps between these two entities will require delicate negotiation and a careful balance of interests.

Furthermore, Taiwan's political status has implications for its national security and defense strategies. As a renegade Chinese province, Taiwan faces constant military threats from the mainland, necessitating a robust defense posture and close cooperation with its allies. Balancing the need for security with the imperative of maintaining stability in the region remains a delicate task for Taiwanese policymakers.

In conclusion, Taiwan's democratic achievements are commendable, but challenges persist in its pursuit of full democratic consolidation. The country's political status as a renegade Chinese province has far-reaching implications for its international relations, security concerns, cultural identity, economic cooperation, and technological advancements. Addressing these challenges requires a multifaceted approach that leverages Taiwan's democratic values and resilient spirit to navigate the complex geopolitical landscape. As Taiwan continues to strive for recognition and independence, the preservation of human rights, the promotion of democracy, and the pursuit of sustainable development will remain central to its future.

International perspectives on Taiwan's human rights and democracy

International perspectives on Taiwan's human rights and democracy play a crucial role in understanding the complexities of its political status. As Taiwan navigates between being a renegade Chinese province or an independent country, the progress and challenges of human rights and democracy in the region take center stage.

From an international standpoint, diplomats, economists, strategists, educators, historians, and the public must closely examine Taiwan's human rights record. The international community has witnessed Taiwan's commitment to upholding democratic principles and safeguarding human rights, even in the face of political adversity. Taiwan's democratic system, with its free and fair elections, independent judiciary, and respect for civil liberties, stands as a beacon of hope in the region.

However, challenges persist in ensuring the full realization of human rights in Taiwan. While significant strides have been made, there is still work to be done to address issues such as gender inequality, labor rights, and the rights of minority groups. International perspectives can provide valuable insights and recommendations to further strengthen Taiwan's human rights framework.

Moreover, international support and recognition for Taiwan's democracy are instrumental in promoting global stability. By acknowledging Taiwan's achievements and advocating for its inclusion in international organizations, the international community can contribute to the advancement of human rights and democracy not only in Taiwan but also in the wider region.

In the context of Taiwan's political status, the international community's perspective on human rights and democracy becomes even more critical. As Taiwan faces pressure and threats from mainland China, the international community must actively support and defend Taiwan's democratic values and human rights. This support can take various forms, including diplomatic engagement, economic cooperation, and strategic alliances.

For diplomats, economists, strategists, educators, historians, and the public, understanding and promoting human rights and democracy in Taiwan is vital for the region's stability and prosperity. By encouraging dialogue, fostering international cooperation, and advocating for Taiwan's rightful place on the global stage, we can contribute to a future where Taiwan's human rights and democracy are fully recognized and respected, regardless of its political status.

In conclusion, international perspectives on Taiwan's human rights and democracy are essential for a comprehensive understanding of its political status. The international community's support and recognition of Taiwan's achievements in promoting human rights and democracy can contribute to the region's stability and prosperity. By actively engaging with Taiwan, the global community can help shape a future where human rights and democracy flourish, regardless of Taiwan's political status as a renegade Chinese province or an independent country.

Social Integration: The Integration of Mainland Chinese and Taiwanese Societies in the Event of Taiwan Becoming an Independent Country

In the complex and ever-evolving landscape of Taiwan's political status, one of the key aspects that demands attention is the social integration of mainland Chinese and Taiwanese societies in the event of Taiwan becoming an independent country. This subchapter delves into the potential challenges and opportunities that lie in the path towards creating a harmonious and inclusive society in this scenario.

Social integration is a multifaceted process that goes beyond mere political and economic considerations. It requires the bridging of cultural, linguistic, and historical gaps to foster mutual understanding, respect, and cooperation. As Taiwan moves towards independence, it must address these challenges head-on to ensure a smooth transition and a cohesive society.

Historically, mainland China and Taiwan have had distinct social, cultural, and political identities. However, the prospect of Taiwan becoming an independent country brings with it the need to forge new ties and connections with mainland Chinese society. This process will require an open and inclusive approach, where dialogue and exchange are encouraged, and commonalities are emphasized over differences.

Education will play a crucial role in facilitating social integration. By promoting cross-cultural understanding and awareness, educational institutions can equip future generations with the necessary tools to navigate a changing landscape. Curricula should include modules on the histories, cultures, and perspectives of both mainland China and Taiwan to foster empathy and mutual respect.

Moreover, initiatives that promote people-to-people exchanges, cultural events, and joint projects can serve as catalysts for social integration. By creating platforms for interaction and dialogue, these activities can help break down barriers and build bridges between mainland Chinese and Taiwanese societies.

However, it is essential to approach social integration with caution, ensuring that it does not lead to the assimilation or erosion of Taiwanese culture. The preservation and promotion of Taiwanese cultural identity should be a priority, even as integration efforts progress. By celebrating and safeguarding their unique heritage, Taiwanese society can maintain its distinctiveness while embracing the benefits of integration.

In conclusion, the social integration of mainland Chinese and Taiwanese societies in the event of Taiwan becoming an independent country is a task that requires careful consideration and planning. By fostering dialogue, promoting education, and celebrating cultural diversity, Taiwan can create a society that is inclusive, harmonious, and resilient. This subchapter provides insights into the challenges and opportunities that lie ahead on this journey towards a unified and integrated Taiwan.

Historical and cultural differences between mainland China and Taiwan

The historical and cultural differences between mainland China and Taiwan have played a significant role in shaping the current political status of Taiwan. These differences have also influenced various aspects of Taiwanese society, including its economic future, international relations, security concerns, cultural identity, human rights and democracy, social integration, economic cooperation, technological advancements, and environmental sustainability.

Historically, Taiwan was colonized by various foreign powers, including the Dutch, Spanish, and Japanese, before becoming a part of the Qing Dynasty in the 17th century. However, after the Chinese Civil War in 1949, the Communist Party of China emerged victorious, establishing the People's Republic of China (PRC) on the mainland, while the defeated Kuomintang (KMT) retreated to Taiwan, where they continued to govern under the name Republic of China (ROC).

This division led to stark contrasts in political ideology, governance, and societal values between the two regions. Mainland China adopted a communist system, characterized by central planning, state ownership, and strict control over political and social activities. In contrast, Taiwan embarked on a path towards democratization, embracing free-market capitalism, individual freedoms, and human rights.

Culturally, Taiwan developed a unique identity over time, drawing influences from its indigenous people, as well as the various colonizers. This cultural amalgamation is evident in Taiwanese cuisine, language, arts, and festivals. In contrast, mainland China has a rich history of its own, with distinct traditions, dialects, and cultural practices that have evolved over thousands of years.

These historical and cultural differences have had profound implications for the political status of Taiwan. Mainland China views Taiwan as a renegade province that must be reunified with the PRC, while Taiwan sees itself as a separate and independent country. This fundamental disagreement has fueled tensions between the two sides and has influenced their diplomatic relations with other countries.

Despite these differences, there have been ongoing efforts to foster economic cooperation and trade partnerships between Taiwan and other countries. Taiwan has emerged as a global economic powerhouse, known for its technological advancements and innovation. Its political status, whether as a renegade Chinese province or an independent country, has not hindered its economic potential and has presented both opportunities and challenges for its future development.

Furthermore, the preservation and promotion of Taiwanese culture have been of utmost importance to the people of Taiwan. In the face of its renegade Chinese province status, Taiwan has made concerted efforts to safeguard its unique cultural heritage and promote cultural exchange with the international community.

In conclusion, the historical and cultural differences between mainland China and Taiwan have shaped the current political status of Taiwan, influencing various aspects of its society. These differences have presented both challenges and opportunities for Taiwan's future as either a renegade Chinese province or an independent country. Understanding these differences is crucial for diplomats, economists, strategists, educators, historians, and the public in comprehending the complexities surrounding Taiwan's political status and its implications for the future.

Social integration challenges and opportunities

Social integration is a crucial aspect to consider in the context of Taiwan's political status as a renegade Chinese province or an independent country. The challenges and opportunities that arise from this issue have far-reaching implications for diplomats, economists, strategists, educators, historians, and the general public.

One of the main challenges of social integration lies in bridging the gap between mainland Chinese and Taiwanese societies. Historically, these two regions have developed distinct cultural, linguistic, and political identities. If Taiwan were to become an independent country, efforts would need to be made to foster understanding, dialogue, and cooperation between these societies. It would require an open and inclusive approach to address any existing tensions and promote mutual respect.

However, social integration also presents opportunities for Taiwan. By embracing its unique cultural identity and promoting it on the global stage, Taiwan can strengthen its position as a distinct entity. It can showcase its vibrant cultural heritage, promote its democratic values, and highlight its achievements in human rights. These efforts can not only enhance Taiwan's international standing but also contribute to the preservation and promotion of Taiwanese culture.

Moreover, social integration has direct implications for the economic cooperation and trade partnerships that Taiwan can forge with other countries. As an independent country, Taiwan can establish its own economic policies, attract foreign investment, and negotiate trade agreements that are tailored to its specific needs. This would enable Taiwan to fully leverage its technological advancements and foster innovation, propelling its economic growth and development.

Furthermore, social integration is closely linked to the progress and challenges of human rights and democracy in Taiwan. As an independent country, Taiwan would have the opportunity to further advance its democratic institutions and protect the rights of its citizens. It would also be able to actively engage with international organizations to promote human rights globally, drawing on its own experiences and achievements in this domain.

In conclusion, social integration poses both challenges and opportunities for Taiwan in the context of its political status. It requires a delicate balance of preserving cultural identity while fostering cooperation and understanding with mainland China. However, social integration also opens doors for economic growth, technological advancements, and the promotion of human rights and democracy. By addressing these challenges and seizing these opportunities, Taiwan can shape a future that is prosperous, inclusive, and aligned with its own aspirations.

Case studies of social integration processes in other contexts

In examining the future of Taiwan's political status and its potential transformation from a renegade Chinese province to an independent country, it is essential to explore case studies of social integration processes in other contexts. By examining the experiences of other regions and nations, Taiwan can gain valuable insights into the challenges and opportunities that lie ahead.

One relevant case study is the reunification of Germany after the fall of the Berlin Wall. The integration of East and West Germany was a complex process, requiring not only political and economic reforms but also social integration. The German experience can provide valuable lessons for Taiwan on how to address issues of national identity, cultural differences, and social cohesion.

Another case study worth considering is the integration of Hong Kong and Macau into China. Both regions were former colonies with distinct cultural and political identities. The process of integrating these regions into the Chinese mainland has had varying degrees of success. Taiwan can learn from the successes and failures of this integration process, particularly in terms of preserving cultural heritage and maintaining a sense of autonomy.

Similarly, the experiences of other former colonies that achieved independence can offer insights into the challenges and opportunities that Taiwan may face. Countries like Singapore, India, and South Africa have had to grapple with issues of national identity, cultural diversity, and social integration. By studying these cases, Taiwan can gain a deeper understanding of the complexities involved in transitioning from a renegade Chinese province to an independent country.

Furthermore, examining social integration processes in multi-ethnic and multicultural societies such as Canada, Australia, and the United States can provide valuable lessons for Taiwan. These countries have successfully managed diverse populations with different cultural backgrounds, languages, and traditions. Taiwan can draw upon their experiences to develop strategies for fostering social cohesion and promoting inclusivity.

By analyzing these case studies, Taiwan can gain a comprehensive understanding of the challenges, opportunities, and best practices in social integration processes. This knowledge can inform policy decisions, guide diplomacy, and shape the future of Taiwan as either a renegade Chinese province or an independent country. It is crucial for diplomats, economists, strategists, educators, historians, and the general public to study and discuss these case studies to ensure a well-informed and holistic approach to Taiwan's future.

Navigating social integration while preserving Taiwanese identity

In the face of its renegade Chinese province status, Taiwan is confronted with the task of navigating social integration while preserving its unique identity. This subchapter delves into the challenges and opportunities that arise in the event of Taiwan becoming an independent country, particularly in terms of cultural preservation and the integration of mainland Chinese and Taiwanese societies.

Taiwanese identity is deeply rooted in its rich cultural heritage, which must be safeguarded and promoted amidst the pressure of assimilation. As Taiwan moves towards independence, it becomes crucial to develop strategies that protect and celebrate the distinct Taiwanese culture. This involves the preservation of language, traditions, and historical narratives that have shaped Taiwanese society for centuries.

Social integration between mainland Chinese and Taiwanese societies presents an additional layer of complexity. While both share a common heritage, they have evolved separately under different political systems and ideologies. It is imperative to foster understanding, mutual respect, and dialogue between these two societies to bridge the gaps that exist and build a harmonious future.

Education plays a vital role in this process, as it cultivates an understanding of Taiwan's unique culture and history among both mainland Chinese and Taiwanese citizens. By incorporating curricula that promote cultural exchange and mutual understanding, educational institutions can foster empathy and bridge the divide between these two societies.

Furthermore, a vibrant civil society can serve as a catalyst for social integration while preserving Taiwanese identity. Non-governmental organizations, community initiatives, and grassroots movements can facilitate dialogue and cooperation between mainland Chinese and Taiwanese individuals, fostering a sense of shared purpose and common values.

To achieve successful social integration, it is essential to create platforms that encourage interaction and cross-cultural exchange. Cultural festivals, art exhibitions, and sports events can serve as avenues for mainland Chinese and Taiwanese citizens to engage with one another, fostering a sense of unity and shared identity.

Ultimately, navigating social integration while preserving Taiwanese identity requires a delicate balance. Taiwan must recognize the importance of embracing diversity while safeguarding its unique heritage. By promoting cultural preservation, fostering social integration, and strengthening educational initiatives, Taiwan can successfully navigate the complexities of the future while preserving its distinct identity.

This subchapter serves as a comprehensive guide for diplomats, economists, strategists, educators, historians, and the general public to understand the challenges and opportunities that arise in the process of social integration while preserving Taiwanese identity. It offers insights into the strategies that can be implemented to ensure a harmonious future for Taiwan as it progresses towards independence.

Economic Cooperation: The Potential for Economic Cooperation and Trade Partnerships between Taiwan and Other Countries as a Renegade Chinese Province or an Independent Country

Taiwan, a region with a complex political status, has long been a key player in the global economy. As discussions continue on whether Taiwan should remain a renegade Chinese province or become an independent country, it is crucial to explore the potential for economic cooperation and trade partnerships that could arise from either scenario.

As a renegade Chinese province, Taiwan would face certain challenges in terms of economic cooperation. However, its robust industrial and technological sectors, as well as its highly skilled workforce, would continue to make it an attractive trade partner for many countries around the world. While diplomatic limitations would exist, Taiwan could still seek to forge economic alliances through various channels, such as bilateral agreements or participation in international organizations.

On the other hand, if Taiwan were to become an independent country, it would gain greater sovereignty and flexibility in its economic endeavors. As an independent nation, Taiwan could negotiate its own trade agreements, establish diplomatic relations, and participate in global fora.

This newfound freedom could potentially open up opportunities for increased foreign investment, expanded export markets, and enhanced economic integration with the global community.

Regardless of its political status, Taiwan's strategic location in East Asia remains a significant advantage. Its proximity to major economies such as China, Japan, and South Korea provides ample opportunities for cross-border trade and investment. Taiwan's expertise in high-tech industries and its advanced infrastructure make it an ideal partner for countries seeking to tap into Asia's growing market.

Furthermore, Taiwan's commitment to innovation and research and development has propelled it to the forefront of technological advancements. This expertise could be leveraged to foster collaborations with other countries, leading to knowledge exchange, joint research projects, and the development of cutting-edge industries.

It is important for diplomats, economists, strategists, educators, historians, and the public to closely examine the potential benefits and challenges associated with economic cooperation between Taiwan and other countries, irrespective of its political status. By fostering dialogue and exploring avenues for collaboration, Taiwan can continue to play a crucial role in the global economy, contributing to regional stability and prosperity.

In conclusion, the potential for economic cooperation and trade partnerships between Taiwan and other countries is significant, regardless of its political status as a renegade Chinese province or an independent country. Taiwan's economic strengths, strategic location, technological advancements, and commitment to innovation make it an attractive partner for international collaboration. By embracing economic cooperation, Taiwan can enhance its global standing and contribute to the sustainable development and prosperity of the region.

Current economic cooperation under renegade Chinese province status

The current economic cooperation under Taiwan's renegade Chinese province status is a topic of immense importance and interest not only to diplomats and economists but also to strategists, educators, historians, and the general public. Taiwan's political status as a renegade Chinese province has created both opportunities and challenges for its economic future.

Despite its uncertain political status, Taiwan has managed to establish itself as a global economic powerhouse. It has become a hub for high-tech manufacturing, a leader in semiconductor production, and a major player in international trade. The island's economic success can be attributed to its skilled workforce, innovative industries, and robust infrastructure.

However, Taiwan's renegade Chinese province status poses certain obstacles to its economic growth. One of the main challenges is the limited access to international markets and trade agreements. Due to the pressure exerted by China, many countries are reluctant to establish formal diplomatic relations with Taiwan, hindering its ability to negotiate trade deals on a global scale.

Nevertheless, Taiwan has been actively seeking alternative avenues for economic cooperation. It has focused on strengthening economic ties with like-minded countries and expanding its trade partnerships. One example is the New Southbound Policy, which aims to deepen economic integration with Southeast Asian nations, South Asia, and Australia and New Zealand.

Furthermore, Taiwan has been actively promoting its participation in regional and international organizations. Despite being excluded from the United Nations and other international bodies, Taiwan has managed to establish informal relationships with various countries and organizations. It has also sought to participate in regional economic initiatives such as the Comprehensive and Progressive Agreement for Trans-Pacific Partnership (CPTPP).

The potential for economic cooperation and trade partnerships between Taiwan and other countries remains significant. Taiwan's technological advancements, skilled workforce, and vibrant entrepreneurial ecosystem make it an attractive partner for many nations. By leveraging its strengths and actively engaging with the international community, Taiwan can continue to foster economic cooperation and build mutually beneficial relationships.

In conclusion, the current economic cooperation under Taiwan's renegade Chinese province status is a complex and dynamic issue. While challenges exist, Taiwan has demonstrated resilience and adaptability in navigating the international economic landscape. By actively seeking alternative avenues for economic cooperation and leveraging its strengths, Taiwan can secure its economic future and continue to thrive as a renegade Chinese province.

Opportunities and challenges for economic cooperation as an independent country

As Taiwan contemplates its future as either a renegade Chinese province or an independent country, the potential opportunities and challenges for economic cooperation become a crucial consideration. This subchapter explores the various aspects of Taiwan's economic future and the implications of its political status on its ability to engage in global trade partnerships.

As an independent country, Taiwan would have the opportunity to forge its own trade agreements and establish economic cooperation with countries around the world. With its advanced technological industries, strong manufacturing base, and highly skilled workforce, Taiwan has the potential to become a key player in the global market. By leveraging its strengths in areas such as semiconductor manufacturing, information technology, and biotechnology, Taiwan can attract foreign investments and secure lucrative trade partnerships.

However, the path to economic independence is not without challenges. Taiwan's political status has a direct impact on its ability to participate in international organizations and negotiate trade agreements. As a renegade Chinese province, Taiwan faces diplomatic challenges as many countries adhere to the "One China" policy, recognizing the People's Republic of China as the legitimate representative of China. This limits Taiwan's access to international markets and hampers its economic potential.

Furthermore, Taiwan's economic integration with mainland China presents both opportunities and risks. As an independent country, Taiwan can benefit from increased economic cooperation with its mainland counterpart. However, it also faces the challenge of balancing its economic ties with China while safeguarding its own national security and sovereignty. Striking the right balance is crucial to ensure that Taiwan's economic cooperation with China does not compromise its position as an independent nation.

Another challenge lies in the preservation and promotion of Taiwanese culture amidst its renegade Chinese province status. Taiwan's cultural identity is a unique asset that can be leveraged to attract tourists, promote cultural exchanges, and stimulate economic growth. However, the threat of cultural assimilation from mainland China poses a significant challenge to the preservation of Taiwanese heritage.

In conclusion, Taiwan's political status as either a renegade Chinese province or an independent country has far-reaching implications for its economic future. While there are opportunities for economic cooperation and trade partnerships, challenges such as diplomatic barriers, balancing economic ties with China, and preserving cultural identity must be carefully navigated. By addressing these challenges and leveraging its strengths, Taiwan can position itself as a thriving independent nation with a strong economy and a distinct cultural identity.

Case studies of successful economic partnerships

In examining the future of Taiwan, it is essential to explore the potential for successful economic partnerships that could shape its destiny as either a renegade Chinese province or an independent country. This subchapter will delve into case studies that highlight the opportunities and challenges that lie ahead.

One notable case study is Taiwan's economic partnership with Japan. Over the years, these two nations have developed a robust trade relationship, with Japan being Taiwan's third-largest trading partner. This partnership has flourished due to shared values, technological advancements, and a mutual commitment to open markets. Japan has been instrumental in supporting Taiwan's economic development, particularly in the fields of technology and innovation. The collaboration between Taiwanese and Japanese companies has resulted in the creation of cutting-edge products that have gained international recognition.

Another case study revolves around Taiwan's economic ties with the United States. Despite the complex political situation, Taiwan and the US have forged a strong economic partnership. The US is Taiwan's second-largest trading partner, and the economic cooperation between the two nations has been instrumental in driving Taiwan's economic growth. The US has provided Taiwan with access to its vast market, while Taiwan has been a vital source of high-quality technology products for American consumers. This partnership has not only bolstered Taiwan's economy but also enhanced its global status as a technological powerhouse.

Furthermore, Taiwan's economic collaboration with European countries has also yielded significant benefits. The European Union (EU) has played a pivotal role in expanding trade and investment opportunities for Taiwan. The EU is Taiwan's fourth-largest trading partner, with bilateral trade increasing steadily over the years. The partnership has been mutually beneficial, with Taiwanese companies gaining access to the European market, and European businesses benefiting from Taiwan's technological expertise. This economic cooperation has also facilitated the exchange of knowledge and best practices in various sectors, contributing to the overall growth and development of both parties.

These case studies demonstrate the potential for Taiwan to develop successful economic partnerships regardless of its political status. Whether as a renegade Chinese province or an independent country, Taiwan's economic future hinges on its ability to forge strong alliances and leverage its technological prowess. By fostering such partnerships, Taiwan can secure its place in the global economy and ensure a prosperous future for its people.

This subchapter aims to provide valuable insights into the economic opportunities and challenges that Taiwan faces, urging policymakers, diplomats, economists, and strategists to consider the potential benefits of economic cooperation and trade partnerships. By examining successful case studies, readers will gain a deeper understanding of how Taiwan can navigate its economic future, regardless of its political status.

Global economic implications and considerations

The political status of Taiwan has significant global economic implications that need to be carefully considered. This subchapter explores the opportunities and challenges that Taiwan faces as either a renegade Chinese province or an independent country. It delves into the potential impact on international relations, security concerns, cultural identity, human rights and democracy, social integration, economic cooperation, technological advancements, and environmental sustainability.

From an economic perspective, Taiwan's political status plays a crucial role in shaping its future. As a renegade Chinese province, Taiwan faces limitations in its ability to engage in international trade and form economic partnerships. On the other hand, as an independent country, it can enjoy greater autonomy to negotiate trade agreements and attract foreign investment.

The impact on international relations is profound. Taiwan's political status affects its diplomatic relations with other countries, particularly those that have strong ties with China. Many nations are forced to make a delicate balance between their economic interests and political allegiances when dealing with Taiwan.

There are also security concerns associated with Taiwan's political status. As a renegade Chinese province, Taiwan has to navigate complex defense strategies to safeguard its national security. However, as an independent country, it can develop its own defense policies and collaborate with other nations to ensure its safety.

Cultural identity is another crucial aspect affected by Taiwan's political status. As a renegade Chinese province, Taiwan faces challenges in preserving and promoting its unique Taiwanese culture. However, as an independent country, it can have greater freedom to assert its cultural identity and showcase its rich heritage to the world.

The progress and challenges of human rights and democracy in Taiwan are also influenced by its political status. As a renegade Chinese province, Taiwan may face limitations in its efforts to further strengthen human rights and democracy. However, as an independent country, it can continue to make strides in these areas and serve as a beacon of democracy in East Asia.

The integration of mainland Chinese and Taiwanese societies is an important consideration in the event of Taiwan becoming an independent country. It requires careful planning and policies to ensure a smooth transition and promote social cohesion between the two societies.

Economically, Taiwan has the potential for greater economic cooperation and trade partnerships as an independent country. It can leverage its technological advancements and highly skilled workforce to attract foreign investment and foster innovation.

Technological advancements play a crucial role in shaping Taiwan's future. As a renegade Chinese province or an independent country, Taiwan can harness technology to drive economic growth, enhance its national security, and improve the quality of life for its citizens.

Lastly, Taiwan's political status has implications for its efforts to promote environmental sustainability and conservation. As a renegade Chinese province or an independent country, Taiwan can continue its initiatives to protect the environment and work towards a more sustainable future.

In conclusion, the global economic implications and considerations of Taiwan's political status are far-reaching. It is essential for diplomats, economists, strategists, educators, historians, and the public to carefully analyze the opportunities and challenges faced by Taiwan as either a renegade Chinese province or an independent country. By examining the impact on international relations, security concerns, cultural identity, human rights and democracy, social integration, economic cooperation, technological advancements, and environmental sustainability, a comprehensive understanding of Taiwan's future can be achieved.

Technological Advancements: The Role of Technology in Shaping the Future of Taiwan as a Renegade Chinese Province or an Independent Country

In recent years, technological advancements have played a crucial role in shaping the future of nations across the globe, and Taiwan is no exception. As the debate surrounding Taiwan's political status intensifies, it is essential to examine how technology can influence its trajectory as either a renegade Chinese province or an independent country.

One area where technology has a significant impact is the economy. Taiwan has long been known for its expertise in the semiconductor industry, with companies like TSMC leading the way in chip manufacturing. As a renegade Chinese province, Taiwan would face challenges in maintaining its economic growth and technological leadership due to potential restrictions imposed by mainland China. On the other hand, as an independent country, Taiwan can leverage its technological prowess to attract foreign investments and foster innovation, further bolstering its economic prospects.

Moreover, technology also plays a crucial role in Taiwan's national security and defense strategies. As a renegade Chinese province, Taiwan would be vulnerable to cyber-attacks and infiltration from mainland China. However, as an independent country, Taiwan can invest in advanced cybersecurity measures, develop cutting-edge military technologies, and collaborate with like-minded nations to ensure its sovereignty and security.

The preservation and promotion of Taiwanese culture is another aspect influenced by technology. As a renegade Chinese province, Taiwan may face challenges in preserving its unique cultural identity amidst the influence of mainland China. However, technology can be harnessed to create platforms for cultural exchange, digital archives, and online communities that help preserve Taiwanese traditions and heritage, ensuring its continuity in the face of political pressure.

Furthermore, technology can facilitate communication and integration between mainland Chinese and Taiwanese societies. In the event of Taiwan becoming an independent country, technology can bridge the gap between the two regions, fostering understanding, cooperation, and social integration. Digital platforms, virtual exchanges, and technological collaborations can pave the way for a harmonious relationship between the two societies.

As Taiwan contemplates its political future, it is crucial to acknowledge the transformative role of technology. Whether it remains a renegade Chinese province or becomes an independent country, technology will shape Taiwan's economy, national security, cultural preservation, social integration, and international relations. Embracing technological advancements and leveraging them strategically will undoubtedly be a key factor in shaping Taiwan's future, ensuring its prosperity, and safeguarding its unique identity and values.

Technological advancements in Taiwan's development

Taiwan has emerged as a key player in the global technology landscape, showcasing remarkable advancements that have shaped its future as both a renegade Chinese province and a potential independent country. With a thriving tech industry, Taiwan has become a hub for innovation, research, and development.

One of Taiwan's most significant technological advancements lies in its semiconductor industry. Home to major semiconductor manufacturers like TSMC, Taiwan has established itself as a leader in producing cutting-edge microchips. These chips power a wide range of devices, from smartphones and computers to advanced medical equipment. Taiwan's expertise in this field has enabled it to maintain a competitive edge in the global market, attracting investments and fostering economic growth.

Furthermore, Taiwan's commitment to research and development has resulted in breakthroughs in various fields. The country has invested heavily in biotechnology, nanotechnology, and renewable energy, positioning itself as a pioneer in these sectors. Advances in biotechnology have led to significant breakthroughs in healthcare, including the development of personalized medicine and innovative treatments for diseases. Taiwan's focus on renewable energy has also been instrumental in promoting environmental sustainability, with the country becoming a leader in solar panel manufacturing.

In addition to its technological achievements, Taiwan has also fostered a conducive environment for startups and entrepreneurship. The government has implemented policies and initiatives to support the growth of tech startups, providing funding, mentorship programs, and access to resources. This has led to the emergence of a vibrant startup ecosystem, attracting talent and investment from around the world.

The technological advancements in Taiwan have not only shaped its economic future but also influenced its international relations. As Taiwan continues to innovate and excel in technology, it has garnered recognition and respect from other nations. This has afforded Taiwan opportunities to develop stronger diplomatic relations and trade partnerships, showcasing its potential as a valuable global player.

However, Taiwan's technological advancements also come with challenges. As a renegade Chinese province, Taiwan faces political pressures and limitations in terms of international cooperation and participation in certain global organizations. It must navigate these challenges while continuing to innovate and adapt to the rapidly evolving technological landscape.

In conclusion, Taiwan's technological advancements have played a crucial role in shaping its future as both a renegade Chinese province and a potential independent country. These advancements have propelled Taiwan to the forefront of the global technology industry, enabling economic growth, fostering international relations, and promoting environmental sustainability. However, as Taiwan seeks to navigate its political status, it must continue to overcome challenges and leverage its technological prowess to secure a prosperous future.

The impact of political status on technological innovation and research

In today's rapidly changing world, technological innovation and research have become crucial factors in determining a country's economic growth and global competitiveness. This holds true for Taiwan, a country that has made significant strides in the field of technology despite its complex political status.

Taiwan's political status as a renegade Chinese province has had a profound impact on its technological advancements. As a province, Taiwan has faced numerous challenges in terms of accessing global resources and technology transfer. It has been excluded from participating in international organizations and agreements, limiting its ability to collaborate with other countries on research and development projects. Additionally, the political tensions between Taiwan and China have hindered the flow of knowledge and talent between the two regions.

However, Taiwan's determination to overcome these obstacles has resulted in impressive technological achievements. Despite its political status, Taiwan has managed to establish a robust research and development ecosystem. The government has invested heavily in science and technology, creating a favorable environment for innovation. Taiwan's renowned semiconductor industry, for example, has played a pivotal role in driving technological advancements not only in Taiwan but also globally.

Moreover, Taiwan's status as a renegade Chinese province has pushed it to diversify its international collaborations. With limited diplomatic recognition, Taiwan has actively sought partnerships with other countries and international organizations. This has led to the establishment of joint research projects, knowledge exchange programs, and technology transfer initiatives. By leveraging its expertise and capabilities, Taiwan has successfully positioned itself as a key player in the global technology arena.

Looking ahead, the future of Taiwan's technological innovation and research will continue to be influenced by its political status. As the country seeks to strengthen its international standing, it will face new opportunities and challenges. Taiwan's ability to navigate the complexities of its political status while fostering technological advancements will be crucial in determining its economic growth and global relevance.

In conclusion, the impact of Taiwan's political status on technological innovation and research cannot be underestimated. Despite being labeled as a renegade Chinese province, Taiwan has demonstrated resilience and determination in advancing its technological capabilities. By investing in research and development, diversifying international collaborations, and leveraging its expertise, Taiwan has managed to overcome the challenges posed by its political status and emerge as a global technology leader. As the country continues to shape its future, the role of technology will undoubtedly play a pivotal role in determining Taiwan's path as either a renegade Chinese province or an independent country.

Technological cooperation and partnerships with other countries

Technological cooperation and partnerships with other countries play a crucial role in shaping the future of Taiwan, whether it remains a renegade Chinese province or achieves independence. As the world becomes increasingly interconnected, Taiwan must leverage its technological capabilities to enhance its global standing and ensure its economic and political viability.

Taiwan has long been recognized as a global leader in technology and innovation. Its thriving tech industry, including giants such as TSMC and Acer, has propelled the country to the forefront of technological advancements. However, Taiwan's political status has posed challenges to its ability to forge international partnerships and fully capitalize on its technological expertise.

In the context of Taiwan's renegade Chinese province status, technological cooperation becomes even more important. By fostering alliances with like-minded countries, Taiwan can gain access to cutting-edge technologies, expand its market reach, and enhance its competitiveness. Collaborative efforts in research and development, particularly in areas such as artificial intelligence, renewable energy, and biotechnology, can drive economic growth and create new opportunities for both Taiwan and its partners.

Moreover, partnerships in technology can also strengthen Taiwan's diplomatic relations. By actively participating in international organizations and initiatives, Taiwan can demonstrate its commitment to global issues and contribute its expertise to global challenges. This, in turn, can help Taiwan gain recognition and support from the international community, bolstering its position on the world stage.

However, the path to technological cooperation and partnerships is not without hurdles. Taiwan's political status has hindered its ability to engage in formal diplomatic relations with many countries. As a result, it must rely on informal channels and creative approaches to forge technological collaborations. Track two diplomacy, academic exchanges, and participation in international conferences are some avenues that Taiwan can explore to foster technological cooperation with other nations.

Furthermore, Taiwan must invest in its domestic technological capabilities to remain competitive in the global landscape. By strengthening its research and development infrastructure, promoting entrepreneurship, and investing in education and talent development, Taiwan can ensure a steady stream of technological innovations and foster an environment conducive to partnerships with other countries.

In conclusion, technological cooperation and partnerships hold immense potential for Taiwan's future, regardless of its political status. By actively seeking collaborations with other nations, Taiwan can enhance its technological capabilities, strengthen its diplomatic relations, and drive economic growth. As Taiwan navigates the complex dynamics of its political status, technology will undoubtedly play a pivotal role in shaping its future as a renegade Chinese province or an independent country.

Harnessing technology for economic growth and national security

In today's interconnected world, technology plays a crucial role in shaping the economic growth and national security of nations. Taiwan, with its unique political status, stands at a crossroads where harnessing technology becomes even more critical for its future as either a renegade Chinese province or an independent country. This subchapter explores the potential of technology in driving Taiwan's economic growth and ensuring its national security.

As a renegade Chinese province, Taiwan faces numerous challenges in its quest for economic prosperity. However, technology presents a unique opportunity for Taiwan to overcome these challenges and carve a niche for itself on the global stage. By investing in research and development, Taiwan can foster innovation and develop cutting-edge technologies that can drive economic growth. This not only boosts domestic industries but also enhances Taiwan's competitiveness in the international market.

Moreover, technology plays a pivotal role in ensuring national security. As Taiwan faces potential threats from its powerful neighbor, it must leverage technology to build a robust defense system. By investing in advanced cyber defense, surveillance systems, and military technologies, Taiwan can strengthen its national security capabilities and deter potential aggressors. Additionally, technological advancements can improve intelligence gathering and enable quick responses to emerging threats, ensuring the safety and sovereignty of the nation.

Furthermore, technology also plays a vital role in promoting environmental sustainability, an issue of global significance. Taiwan, with its political status, must navigate complex international relations to address environmental challenges effectively. By harnessing technology for renewable energy, waste management, and conservation efforts, Taiwan can demonstrate its commitment to environmental sustainability. This not only enhances its global reputation but also contributes to a greener future for the nation and the world.

In conclusion, technology is a powerful tool that can shape the future of Taiwan, regardless of its political status. By harnessing technology for economic growth, national security, environmental sustainability, and cultural preservation, Taiwan can position itself as a forward-thinking nation on the global stage. It is imperative for diplomats, economists, strategists, educators, historians, and the public to recognize the potential of technology in shaping Taiwan's future and work towards maximizing its benefits. Only then can Taiwan truly unlock its potential and secure a prosperous and secure future, whether as a renegade Chinese province or an independent country.

Environmental Sustainability: The Impact of Taiwan's Political Status on its Efforts to Promote Environmental Sustainability and Conservation

Environmental sustainability is a critical issue that affects countries around the world, and Taiwan is no exception. However, Taiwan's political status as a renegade Chinese province has significant implications for its efforts to promote environmental sustainability and conservation.

One of the main challenges that Taiwan faces in this regard is its limited international recognition and participation in global environmental initiatives. As a renegade province, Taiwan is not a member of the United Nations and is unable to fully participate in international agreements and organizations related to environmental sustainability. This hampers Taiwan's ability to access funding, resources, and technical expertise necessary to implement effective environmental policies and initiatives.

Furthermore, Taiwan's political status also affects its ability to forge international partnerships and collaborations on environmental issues. Many countries are hesitant to engage in environmental cooperation with Taiwan due to concerns over its political status and China's influence. This limits Taiwan's opportunities for knowledge sharing, technology transfer, and joint research projects, which are crucial for addressing complex environmental challenges.

Despite these challenges, Taiwan has made significant efforts to promote environmental sustainability and conservation within its own borders. The government has implemented various policies and initiatives to reduce carbon emissions, promote renewable energy sources, and conserve natural resources. Taiwan has also invested in environmental education and awareness programs to foster a culture of sustainability among its citizens.

Additionally, Taiwan's civil society plays a crucial role in advocating for environmental protection and conservation. Non-governmental organizations, research institutions, and grassroots movements have emerged to fill the gaps left by Taiwan's political isolation and have been instrumental in driving environmental initiatives at the local level.

However, without full recognition and participation on the international stage, Taiwan's efforts to promote environmental sustainability and conservation are limited in their impact. It is crucial for the international community to recognize the importance of Taiwan's contributions to global environmental efforts and to support its inclusion in international organizations and agreements.

In conclusion, Taiwan's political status as a renegade Chinese province has significant implications for its efforts to promote environmental sustainability and conservation. Despite these challenges, Taiwan has shown a strong commitment to environmental protection, but its ability to fully address environmental issues is hampered by its limited international recognition. It is essential for the global community to recognize Taiwan's contributions and support its inclusion in international environmental initiatives for the benefit of the planet as a whole.

Environmental challenges and initiatives in Taiwan

Taiwan, as a renegade Chinese province with a unique political status, faces numerous environmental challenges. However, the country has also made significant strides in implementing initiatives to promote environmental sustainability and conservation.

One of the key environmental challenges in Taiwan is air pollution. Due to rapid industrialization and urbanization, Taiwan has experienced high levels of air pollution, particularly in its major cities. The burning of fossil fuels for energy production, industrial emissions, and vehicular pollution contribute to this problem. In response, the Taiwanese government has implemented various measures to combat air pollution, such as stricter emission standards for vehicles and the promotion of renewable energy sources like solar and wind power.

Another pressing environmental challenge is water pollution. Taiwan's rivers and coastal areas have been heavily polluted by industrial wastewater and agricultural runoff. To address this issue, the government has implemented stricter regulations on industrial wastewater treatment and has promoted organic farming practices to reduce chemical runoff. Additionally, Taiwan has invested in advanced water treatment technologies to improve the quality of its water sources.

Deforestation is also a significant environmental challenge in Taiwan. The country's mountainous regions have been subject to illegal logging and land development, leading to habitat destruction and soil erosion. To combat deforestation, the Taiwanese government has implemented reforestation programs and established protected areas to preserve the country's biodiversity.

In terms of initiatives, Taiwan has launched various programs to promote environmental sustainability. For instance, the government has implemented a recycling system that encourages citizens to sort their waste and has set targets for increasing recycling rates. Furthermore, Taiwan has been investing in renewable energy, particularly solar and wind power, to reduce its reliance on fossil fuels and combat climate change.

Despite these efforts, Taiwan still faces challenges in balancing economic development with environmental conservation. The country's industrial growth and urban expansion have put pressure on its natural resources and ecosystems. Therefore, it is crucial for Taiwan to continue implementing sustainable development practices and promoting environmental awareness among its citizens.

In conclusion, Taiwan faces several environmental challenges as a renegade Chinese province. However, the country has implemented various initiatives to promote environmental sustainability and conservation. By addressing issues such as air and water pollution, deforestation, and promoting renewable energy, Taiwan is taking significant steps towards a greener future. It is essential for Taiwan to continue prioritizing environmental protection as it navigates its unique political status and strives for a sustainable and prosperous future.

Implications of political status on environmental policies and regulations

The implications of Taiwan's political status on environmental policies and regulations are crucial to the future of the country, whether it remains a renegade Chinese province or becomes an independent country. Diplomats, economists, strategists, educators, historians, and the public must understand the significance of this issue for Taiwan's sustainable development.

Under its current renegade Chinese province status, Taiwan faces challenges in implementing effective environmental policies and regulations. As it lacks international recognition, Taiwan is often excluded from global environmental agreements and organizations, limiting its ability to contribute to and benefit from international efforts to address climate change and promote sustainability.

However, Taiwan has shown remarkable resilience in pursuing environmental sustainability despite these limitations. As a small island nation, it has recognized the vulnerability of its ecosystems and has implemented various policies to protect its natural resources. Taiwan has invested in renewable energy sources, such as wind and solar power, and has set ambitious targets to reduce greenhouse gas emissions.

If Taiwan were to become an independent country, it would have greater opportunities to participate in international environmental initiatives. It could establish its own environmental policies and regulations, tailored to its unique context and needs. Taiwan's scientific expertise and technological advancements could contribute to global efforts to combat climate change and promote sustainable development.

Moreover, Taiwan's political status has implications for its ability to address environmental challenges in cross-strait relations. As an independent country, Taiwan could negotiate with China on issues of mutual concern, such as air and water pollution, deforestation, and illegal wildlife trade. Cooperation between the two entities could lead to more effective and comprehensive environmental strategies.

Regardless of its political status, Taiwan must continue to prioritize environmental sustainability and conservation. It must invest in research and innovation, promote public awareness and engagement, and collaborate with international partners to address global environmental issues. Taiwan's unique cultural identity and democratic values can serve as a driving force for environmental stewardship and inspire other nations to adopt sustainable practices.

In conclusion, the political status of Taiwan has significant implications for its environmental policies and regulations. Whether it remains a renegade Chinese province or becomes an independent country, Taiwan must navigate challenges and seize opportunities to promote environmental sustainability. This subchapter aims to shed light on these implications and stimulate informed discussions among diplomats, economists, strategists, educators, historians, and the public.

International cooperation for environmental sustainability

International cooperation for environmental sustainability is a crucial aspect of Taiwan's future, regardless of its political status. As a renegade

Chinese province or an independent country, Taiwan must prioritize environmental protection and work together with the international community to address global challenges such as climate change, pollution, and biodiversity loss.

Taiwan has made significant progress in promoting environmental sustainability in recent years. It has implemented policies to reduce greenhouse gas emissions, increase renewable energy production, and improve waste management. However, due to its political status, Taiwan faces several obstacles in participating fully in international efforts to combat environmental issues.

One major challenge is Taiwan's limited diplomatic relations with other countries. As a result of China's influence, Taiwan is excluded from many international organizations and agreements, hindering its ability to contribute to global environmental initiatives. Therefore, international cooperation is essential to bridge this gap and ensure Taiwan's participation in international environmental efforts.

Collaboration with other countries can bring numerous benefits to Taiwan's environmental sustainability goals. By sharing knowledge, expertise, and resources, Taiwan can learn from the experiences of other nations and implement effective strategies to address environmental challenges. International cooperation can also facilitate technology transfer, allowing Taiwan to adopt innovative solutions for sustainable development.

Furthermore, cooperation with other countries can enhance Taiwan's access to funding for environmental projects. Financial support from international organizations and foreign governments can help Taiwan invest in renewable energy infrastructure, conservation initiatives, and sustainable agriculture practices.

To promote international cooperation for environmental sustainability, Taiwan should actively engage in regional and global forums on climate change, environmental conservation, and biodiversity protection. It should forge partnerships with like-minded countries, organizations, and agencies to jointly address shared environmental concerns.

In conclusion, international cooperation is crucial for Taiwan's efforts to promote environmental sustainability, regardless of its political status. By actively participating in global environmental initiatives, Taiwan can contribute its expertise, learn from others, and access resources to address pressing environmental challenges. Through collaboration with other countries, Taiwan can lay the foundation for a more sustainable future and ensure the well-being of its people and the planet.

Balancing economic development and environmental conservation efforts in the future of Taiwan

As Taiwan looks towards its future, one of the critical challenges it faces is finding the balance between economic development and environmental conservation. This subchapter explores the implications of Taiwan's political status, whether it remains a renegade Chinese province or becomes an independent country, on its ability to address this delicate balance.

Taiwan has achieved remarkable economic growth over the years, establishing itself as a global economic powerhouse. However, this progress has come at a cost to the environment. As a renegade Chinese province, Taiwan's economic policies have often prioritized industrial development over environmental concerns. This has led to pollution, deforestation, and habitat destruction, threatening the island's biodiversity and natural resources.

If Taiwan were to become an independent country, it would have the opportunity to reassess its economic and environmental priorities. With a greater degree of autonomy, Taiwan could implement policies that promote sustainable development, investing in renewable energy sources, green technologies, and eco-friendly practices. This shift towards a more environmentally conscious approach would not only safeguard Taiwan's rich natural heritage but also strengthen its international reputation as a responsible global citizen.

However, the path towards achieving this balance will not be easy. Taiwan's economic future, whether as a renegade Chinese province or an independent country, is closely tied to its trade partnerships and global economic integration. Balancing economic development and environmental conservation will require innovative strategies that foster sustainable growth while minimizing ecological impact. This will necessitate the collaboration of diplomats, economists, and strategists to develop effective policies that promote both economic prosperity and environmental sustainability.

Furthermore, public awareness and education will play a crucial role in shaping Taiwan's future. Educators and historians must emphasize the importance of environmental conservation and sustainable practices, instilling a sense of responsibility towards the environment in future generations. The government should also invest in research and development, supporting scientists and experts in finding innovative solutions to pressing environmental challenges.

In conclusion, striking a balance between economic development and environmental conservation is of paramount importance for the future of Taiwan. Whether it remains a renegade Chinese province or becomes an independent country, Taiwan must prioritize sustainable development, investing in green technologies, and promoting environmentally friendly practices. By doing so, Taiwan can secure its economic prosperity while preserving its natural resources for future generations.